Glory Days INDIANA

LEGENDS OF INDIANA
HIGH SCHOOL BASKETBALL

Dick Denny

D1036563

SP

SPORTS
PUBLISHING
L.L.C.

SportsPublishingLLC.com

ISBN-10: 1-59670-062-9
ISBN-13: 978-1-59670-062-8

Publishers: Peter L. Bannon and Joseph J. Bannon Sr.
Senior managing editor: Susan M. Moyer
Acquisitions editor: Mike Pearson
Developmental editor: Suzanne Perkins
Art director: K. Jeffrey Higgerson
Dust jacket design: Heidi Norsen
Interior design and layout: Jeff Higgerson and Heidi Norsen
Photo editor: Erin Linden-Levy

Sports Publishing L.L.C.
804 North Neil Street
Champaign, IL 61820
Phone: 1-877-424-2665
Fax: 217-363-2073
SportsPublishingLLC.com

Printed in the United States of America

CIP data available upon request

To my late wife Arlene, who grew to love Indiana high school basketball as much as I do. She enjoyed sitting in Hinkle Fieldhouse during the state tournament finals with the other wives of the *Indianapolis News* sports staff members. Arlene was my constant support throughout a long and rewarding journey through Hoosier Hysteria, which is without equal anywhere in the country.

And to the rest of my family: Chris, who cherishes the letter he received from Bob Knight after expressing disappointment that his favorite coach was no longer at his alma mater—Indiana University; Sean, who learned so many valuable lessons through his association with the staff and membership at Crooked Stick Golf Club in Carmel; Tim, a far better catcher than his dad ever was while at North Central High School and IUPUI; and Shannon, who thrilled her mother as a North Central Panther guard for basketball coach Chuck Boehlke.

Thanks kids. You made it easy for your father to complete this tribute to the Glory Days of some of Indiana's finest all-time high school stars.

Respectfully, Dick Denny

To Gene,
  I hope you enjoy
Glory Days as much
as I did putting it
together.
  Long live Hoosier
Hysteria.
          Best wishes,
          Dick Denny

Contents

Acknowledgments vii

Foreword by Bob Hammel viii

George McGinnis 1

Rick Mount 6

Bob Heaton 11

Bryce Drew 15

Carl Erskine 19

Johnny Wilson 23

Bill Shepherd 27

Billy Shepherd 31

Dave Shepherd 35

Hallie Bryant 39

Mike Warren 44

Harley Andrews 49

Arley Andrews 53

Billy Keller 57

Ralph Taylor 62

Brad Miley 67

Eric Montross 71

Larry Humes 75

Don Buse 79

Mike Weaver 84

Dick Dickey 89

Monte Towe 93

Ken Pennington 97

Bob Ford 109

Roger Burkman 114

Pete Trgovich 118

Steve Welmer 123

Chuck DeVoe 127

Ron Bonham 131

Darnell Archey 136

Cam Cameron 141

Dave Colescott 146

Louie Dampier 151

Lee Hamilton 156

Mark Herrmann 160

Mike McCoy 164

Joe Sexson 169

George Crowe 173

Sean May 177

Epilogue 181

Acknowledgments

I have been to the National Basketball Hall of Fame in Springfield, Massachusetts; the National Baseball Hall of Fame in Cooperstown, New York; and the National Football Hall of Fame in Canton, Ohio. To say that the Indiana Basketball Hall of Fame in New Castle compares favorably to these three is an enormous understatement. It is a gem at any level, high school, college or the pros.

Executive Director of the Indiana Hall of Fame Roger Dickinson, his fine staff, and the Hall's many volunteers made me feel at home the minute I stepped into the facility. I owe them a huge debt of gratitude for assisting in my research for this book.

For answering all of my questions I owe special thanks to Pat Aikman, Indiana All-Star game director for the series with Kentucky, and to Joe Gentry, public relations director for the Indiana High School Athletic Association.

Herb Schwomeyer's *Hoosier Hysteria* book and *Total Basketball: The Ultimate Basketball Encyclopedia* were vitally important sources of information. I thank the sports information offices at Indiana State University, the University of Evansville, Purdue University, Indiana University, the University of Louisville, North Carolina State University, and the University of North Carolina. And a special thank you to Susan Davis, university archivist at Indiana State.

Bob Hammel, a former colleague of mine at the *Indianapolis News* sports department before he became the sports editor of the *Bloomington Herald-Telephone*, has always been someone I go to for advice about journalistic matters. He read several of my chapters and advised me to go forward as swiftly as possible with *Glory Days*. I thank him for his valued friendship and encouragement.

And to David Woods of the *Indianapolis Star*, also a former colleague of mine at the *News*. Thanks for encouraging me to tackle this project back in the fall of 2004. It has been a challenge and a joy.

Foreword

By Bob Hammel

Indiana high school basketball is by far the state's most productive source of legends. Since the statewide tournament began nearly a full century ago, players from all parts of Hoosierland have been showing off their best. In the decade that started with the selection of the first Indiana high school basketball champion (1911), the tournament spotlighted the sport's first truly great big man, Homer Stonebraker of Wingate's back-to-back champions in 1913 and 1914; and another name never removed from all-time-best consideration, Fuzzy Vandivier of Franklin's three-time-champion "Wonder Five." Star production never slowed in Indiana high school basketball.

This book introduces some of those more modern legendary stars to a new generation of readership, while allowing some of those other generations to renew their familiarity with stars of their own day. It even gives those who thought they knew about some of them a look at their lives that isn't so generally familiar.

You know, for example, of Carl Erskine, Indiana's contribution to the pitching staff of the 1940s and '50s Brooklyn Dodgers teams given their own niche of immortality by Roger Kahn's all-time bestseller, *The Boys of Summer*. You know of his world series-record 13-strikeout game—13 Mickey Mantle-era Yankees in 1953—and of the man Brooklyn lovingly called "Oiskin" who pitched two no-hit games. Read inside these pages and you'll know much more about the basketball Carl Erskine, from Anderson High, and the post-baseball Carl, a growingly more admirable man as he advances in years.

There'll be no cherry-picking here, no more picking out of a choice name or two. There are nuggets for you to find in every one-time Hoosier star whom Dick has brought back here for an encore.

The neat thing is we poets of the press box will never run out of personalities to introduce and re-introduce to you. But few will ever do it with the entertaining touch and the grace of Dick Denny, in the stories he gives you here.

I don't have to say, "Enjoy!"

You will.

George McGinnis

Washington High School, Indianapolis

Year graduated
1969

Major accomplishments
Scored a record 148 points in the final four games of the '69 state tournament; First Indiana high school player to score more than 1,000 points (1,019) in a season; Set the record of 53 points and 31 rebounds in the second game of the Indiana-Kentucky All-Star series; Mr. Basketball; Named one of Indiana's all-time 50 best players in 1999; Named a Living Legend by the Indiana Historical Society; Indiana Basketball Hall of Famer

George McGinnis, whose retired No. 30 Indiana Pacers jersey hangs from the Conseco Fieldhouse rafters in Indianapolis, vividly remembers looking up at his 6-foot-7 father, Burnie, as a young boy, and listening to him talk about the Attucks High School team that won successive state championships in 1955 and '56.

"I didn't really understand the implications of what it all meant," admits the 6-foot-8, 235-pounder who became Indiana Mr. Basketball in 1969 after helping Washington High School become the third team to win the state championship with an unbeaten record.

"But I saw the joy those victories produced when I walked outside and witnessed people celebrating. There were two significant eras that had a profound effect on what we now consider Hoosier Hysteria. One, obviously, was Milan in 1954. And certainly I think those Attucks teams in '55 and '56 brought a sense of pride to the African American community in the Indianapolis area."

After witnessing the 1955 Attucks team—the first all-black school in the country to win a state title, which made them the first Indianapolis champion—join Milan in the Indiana Basketball Hall of Fame in March, 2005, McGinnis said, "There was Milan, and then God said, 'Let there be Attucks.'"

McGinnis believes that "Oscar Robertson of those two Attucks teams is, if not the greatest, then one of the top three players that ever played basketball."

When asked if the '69 Washington team could beat the '56 Attucks team, the first unbeaten state champion, McGinnis chuckled and said, "Boy, that would have been a tough game. I'd just like to stand on my 31-0 and let them stand at their 31-0."

Apparently, God also said, "Let there be George McGinnis and Indianapolis Washington." Utilizing his sculpted frame, McGinnis became a three-time Parade All-American in football, and a two-time *Parade* All-American in basketball in high school. His football coach, Bob Springer, claimed that McGinnis was "the best football player I had ever seen."

Of the nearly 400 recruiting letters McGinnis received, close to 55 percent were offers for football. However, late in McGinnis' senior year in high school, basketball became his passion, as well as his ticket to fame and considerable fortune.

His journey to greatness received a major boost in the '68-'69 season when he became the first Indiana high school player to score more than 1,000 points (1,019 for a 32.8 average); breaking Lewisville's Marion Pierce's 1960-61 record of 972 (Dave Shepherd of Carmel currently holds the record of 1,079 set in 1970). McGinnis also scored 148 points in the final four games of the state tournament, a record that still stands.

Three of the four teams in the 1969 Final Four at Hinkle Fieldhouse were undefeated: Washington (29-0), Marion (27-0), and Vincennes (27-0). Gary Tolleston had lost only once (27-1). The day was filled with controversy. A blown fuse in an unreachable place under the floor put the time clock out of commission, and officials had to keep time with a windup clock in the two afternoon games and through a good part of the championship game.

The biggest controversy occurred in the first quarter of Washington's afternoon game against Marion, which the Continentals finally won with a fourth-quarter rally, 61-60. McGinnis and teammate Steve Downing fought for a rebound, and it appeared to some observers that Downing went over a Marion player's back. Downing raised his hand when a referee called a foul. McGinnis, however, was assessed the foul, and Downing scored the winning basket with 22 seconds remaining. Had that early foul gone to Downing, he would have been out of the game with three minutes left on five fouls.

"I couldn't say 100 percent whether it was my foul or Steve's foul," said McGinnis. "Steve and I both had our hands in there. I'm the one who got the foul, so I'm gonna say the officials made the correct call. We were down eight, 10 points going into the fourth quarter. Our coach [Bill Green] said, 'We're gonna press 'em full court.' We had a 2-1-2 press that we didn't use a great deal during the regular season, only because we were so much better than most teams. We came up with some quick steals and were fortunate to win a very close game." The Continentals defeated Tolleston, 79-76, in the title game.

McGinnis' reputation received an enormous boost during the second game of the Indiana-Kentucky All-Star series in Louisville. McGinnis scored 53 points and grabbed 31 rebounds, both record totals that still stand, as Indiana won two games, 91-83 and 114-83.

"McGinnis' game in Louisville is the best basketball performance I've ever seen," said Bob Hammel, who is in the Indiana Hall of Fame for excellence in basketball writing for the *Bloomington Herald-Telephone*. Hammel covered McGinnis when McGinnis led the Big Ten in scoring with a 29.9 average in his only varsity season (1970-71) at Indiana University.

Recalling the week leading up to his mammoth game in Louisville's Freedom Hall, McGinnis said, "I was Mr. Basketball and had a huge amount of press clippings for breaking a ton of Marion County scoring records. We were the second Indianapolis undefeated team in the history of the tournament, so there were a lot of comparisons between us and the great Oscar Robertson-led Attucks teams.

"I had a very decent game, around 19 points and 10 rebounds, in the opener in Hinkle Fieldhouse. After that game, one of the Kentucky players, Joe Voskuhl, was quoted as saying, 'I hear that this McGinnis has been compared to the great Oscar Robertson, and we didn't feel he was that great at all. There was not even anything very special about him.'

"Our next game in Freedom Hall was sold out. I had probably the greatest basketball game of my life. Voskuhl later made amends for his quote. He called me a few years ago to say he still thought about that stupid remark he made."

McGinnis' decision to attend IU was sealed two weeks after that memorable game in Louisville. His father fell from a scaffold at his construction job and was tragically killed.

"It was kinda ironic," said McGinnis. "I had just turned 18 and the greatest game I ever played [against Kentucky] was the last game my dad saw me play. Needless to say he was very proud. My mother [Willie] had never worked, never drove a car. What she did at home was tremendous and I just thought, based on me going to Indiana, other than I loved the school, loved the tradition; I could be close to home. My mother could come see me play."

Was it the right time for McGinnis to leave IU and sign with the Pacers after just two years there (freshmen weren't eligible for the varsity his first season)? "I do have some regrets about leaving school early," he said. "I wish I could have had the opportunity to play two more years. I remember it would have been my senior year that Indiana played UCLA in the Final Four and got beat by a great UCLA team. I think if I would have been on that IU team it might have made a difference.

"I was a victim of circumstance. I needed to take care of my family. And that's the reason I left. It had nothing to do with basketball. What's neat is that I got a $20,000 signing bonus from the Pacers, and I took that money and bought my mother a house. That's one of the most pleasing things I've done. She's still in that house."

Pro basketball life was just as good to McGinnis as amateur basketball life, except for 1977 when his Philadelphia 76ers team finished runner up to Portland in the NBA championship series. "Seventy-seven was a tough year, because it was the first time I ever experienced losing," he said. "We were favored to win and took the first two games at home, but then lost four in a row. Portland surprised us and played a heck of a lot better than we did."

In his 10-year pro career, McGinnis won two ABA titles with the Pacers (1972 and 1973), was an ABA All-Star first-team selection in 1974 and '75, shared the ABA most valuable player award in 1975 with Julius "Dr. J." Erving, and was NBA first-team in 1976 with Philadelphia.

McGinnis says his days with the Pacers were special. "I came to a team that had great tradition and I played with great teammates: Roger Brown,

Mel Daniels, Freddie Lewis, Bob Netolicky, Darnell Hillman, Billy Keller. One of the great things about that is that we're all still very close today. And we had a character as a coach, Slick Leonard. He was not only a coach, but a father figure. He'd get mad and kinda let you have it, but he'd also go out with you after a game and have dinner.

"I think that Pacer era is what put Indiana professional basketball on the map, and it got its start at the Coliseum. I was really happy to be a part of that."

At the end of the '75 season, McGinnis actually signed with the New York Knicks of the NBA, but the league voided the contract and he wound up with Philadelphia, which had his draft rights.

"It was a financial decision," said McGinnis. "I was making $75,000 or $85,000 with the Pacers, and Philadelphia matched the contract the Knicks gave me [$3.2 million over six years]. I went back to the Pacers and they said they couldn't do it."

Philadelphia traded McGinnis to Denver in 1978. In his second season in Denver, he was dealt to the Pacers, retiring in 1982 at the age of 31. McGinnis still holds several Pacer records: points in a game (58), offensive rebounds in a game (16), total rebounds in a game (37), scoring average for a season (29.8 in 1974-75), and all-time scoring average (19.6).

What has basketball meant to "Big Mac," who was inducted into the Indiana Basketball Hall of Fame in 1995 and in 2004 was named an Indiana living legend by the Indiana Historical Society? "For some guys basketball can be the best thing that ever happened to you," he said. "For other guys it can be the worst thing that happened to you. For me, I can honestly say that without me having the opportunity to play the game, I don't know what I'd be doing now. I don't even know if I'd be living. There weren't a whole lot of heroes in my neighborhood.

"I'm just so happy to come from good stock where I was a big kid and it afforded me the opportunity to not only play but excel. Everything I've ever gotten in life started from just being a basketball player."

McGinnis and his wife, Lynda, have one son, Tony, 36, and one grandson, Dane, 13. McGinnis has excelled for them and his mother for all of his 56 years.

Rick Mount

Lebanon High School, Lebanon

Year graduated
1966

Major accomplishments
Lebanon's all-time leading scorer with 2,595 points for four seasons, and
fourth on the state's all-time list; First high school athlete in a
team sport to be featured on the cover of Sports Illustrated as a
senior; Mr. Basketball; Named one of Indiana's all-time 50 best players
in 1999; Indiana Basketball Hall of Famer

In the summer of 1965, just eight months before *Sports Illustrated* chose
him to be the first high-schooler in a team sport to appear on the cover,
Lebanon's Rick Mount decided to test his skill at a basketball shoot being
held at a Fourth of July fair in the city park. He had already earned the
nickname "The Rocket" because his right-handed release resembled the
launching of a deadly missile.

"When you went over there in your regular clothes you weren't
warmed up," said the three-time All-American at Purdue and five-year pro
in the ABA. "The balls were inflated pretty tight. So I got my basketball stuff
on and warmed up at the outdoor court, then went over to the basketball
shoot. I just wanted to see what I could do warmed up."

Mount not only was warmed up, he was red hot. "I had the guy
running it for 25 Teddy Bears," he chuckled. "I shut him down that night.
People were giving me money to win a Teddy Bear for their kids. Once I got
done, the man said, 'What's your name?' I said, 'Rick Mount.' He said, 'I knew
you were Rick Mount. I should have sat you down right at first.' The guy

said, 'Tomorrow I've got to go to the bank and get some money, so I get some more Teddy Bears.' He wanted to know if I wanted to go on the carnival circuit with him and shoot for money.

"About three years ago a mother brought her kid to one of my shooting camps and she said, 'I'm one of those kids you won a Teddy Bear for.'"

Rick declined the invitation to go on the carnival circuit for obvious reasons.

Mount has been teaching kids how to shoot the last 17 years at his nine Rick Mount Shooting School camps—two in Illinois, one in Ohio, and six in Indiana: two in Indianapolis and four in Fort Wayne. The 800 to 1,000 kids who attend the camps each summer are able to shoot rapidly because of a Shoot-A-Way device attached to the goal. The way it works is that a ball falls into the net after a camper shoots it, and goes down to a hopper, which throws the ball back to the camper.

Rick has a Shoot-A-Way device, called "The Gun," at his home. Mount has been the Indiana rep for the device for 18 years. It takes about two minutes to set up and then Rick fires away. Is he shooting as well as ever?

"When I was younger I got up pretty high on my shot." he said. "Now I can get up pretty good on my shot, but I'm 59 years old. I can make 96 out of 100. That's three-pointers, not free throws. I can hit 100 out of 100 free throws."

In addition to that, Mount averages between 400 and 500 jump shots a day on the goal in the driveway of his modest home in north Lebanon. "People say, 'Mount, you're crazy, what are you trying to do, bring back your career?' I say, 'Why do you go out and run on a street? Why do you ride a stationary bike?' I don't like to do either of those things. I can still shoot jump shots. And it keeps me in shape."

Mount takes pride in being a self-taught jump shooter. He credits his late father, Paul (Pete) Mount, with two major assists in his development (the Mounts are one of the few families to produce three Indiana All-Stars: Pete in 1944, Rick in 1966 and Rich, Rick's son, in 1989—all three started four years for Lebanon, and both Pete and Rick are in the Indiana Basketball Hall of Fame).

"Nobody ever taught me how to shoot," said Mount. "It fell into place. I think it was because my dad didn't start me out with a 10-foot basket and a big ball, where I had to shove it up there. I used a tennis ball on a lower basket."

When Mount was five, Pete cut the bottom out of a Planters Peanuts can and nailed it to the back porch. He started to hit the can with a tennis ball, but he didn't think the can looked like a basket, so he got a coat hanger and straightened it out. He made it about as big around as the Planters can, took two rolls of athletic tape and wrapped it around the hanger to a size about as thick as his thumb so it would be sturdy. He cut up a fishing net to complete the basket.

When the family moved a second time, Rick put his homemade basket in the garage and he would go to the corner, jump up and shoot his tennis ball over the rafters. "That got me to lifting the ball and jumping good when I was young," he said. "I never picked up any bad habits. When I got a little older my dad put up an eight-foot basket outside, and I shot a volleyball at it. I didn't shoot at a 10-foot basket with a regulation ball until I was in the fourth grade."

The silver ring Pete Mount received when Lebanon finished runner-up to Fort Wayne Central in the 1943 state tournament was instrumental in instilling a fiery competitiveness in Mount at age seven. Pete found his son wearing the ring twice during the summer and got into his face both times.

"I never talked back to my dad, because he'd pound me with that ping pong paddle he had," said Mount. "He broke one on me one time. I said, 'Here, take your silver ring. I'm gonna get the gold ring. I'm gonna win the state championship and outdo you.' At that point I was driven."

In Mount's freshman year at Lebanon, under coach Jim Rosenstihl, he averaged 20.5 points a game. The average climbed to 23.5 as a sophomore, to 33.1 as a junior, and finally to 33.2 as a senior. He ranks fourth on the state high school career-scoring list with 2,595 points. When the Tigers lost to East Chicago Washington, 59-58, in the championship game of the West Lafayette semistate in 1966, Mount's dream of winning a gold ring ended.

"Starting the fourth quarter, I always got cramps, in the sectional, regional and semistate," said Mount. "When I got those cramps in the semistate, I had just hit a basket and we were up 15 points. I never put up another shot."

Going to Purdue, after turning down Miami of Florida, meant that Mount could remain true to himself. "I could come home when I wanted to, because Lebanon is only 45 minutes away, and I was far enough away that I felt like I was on my own," he said.

"I had a really great college career. I did some things that put Purdue on the map," said Mount who holds the men's career scoring record with 2,323 points for a 32.3 average, in addition to the men's single-game record of 61. "If you had told me we were going to the final game of the NCAA tournament my junior year the way our chemistry was, I'd have said forget it."

Fortunately, the team spent about two weeks during the holidays together at the Sun Devil Classic and Rainbow Classic. By the time the Big Ten season began, the players started caring for each other. The Boilermakers lost only one conference game, at Ohio State, by three points. In the championship game, Purdue played without center Chuck Bavis, who had suffered a shoulder injury in the Mideast regional. Mount shot horribly in the first half, but recovered well in the second-half; however, it was too late and the Bruins won, 92-72.

"Purdue had Rick Mount, a great player," said UCLA coach John Wooden, himself a former Boilermaker player. "And I had Kenny Heitz, a 6-3 guard, play him. Kenny did a tremendous job of controlling Mount until we had the game well in hand."

Mount hit his first two shots, then missed 14 in a row to be 2-for-16 at the half. He was 10-for-20 the second half, finishing 12-for-36 for the game, scoring 33 points. "Johnny Wooden would like to think that his decision to put Kenny Heitz on me [was a major reason that I shot so poorly the first half)," said Mount. "But that wasn't it. I don't know what really happened in the championship game, the energy and the focus, just boom, from a period of about six minutes gone in the first half for maybe 12 minutes I had nothing going. After the half I come out and everything's back."

Of his five ABA seasons—two with Indiana, which drafted him No. 1 in 1970; a year and a half with Kentucky; a half-year with Utah; and a year with Memphis—Mount says, "People keep saying I had a bad pro career, but I didn't have that bad a pro career. When I got to play a lot of minutes, I had some pretty good numbers. I really take pride in being in three ABA championship finals." These championships took place in 1972 when the Pacers won their second of three titles, 1973 when Kentucky was runner-up to Indiana, and in 1974 when Utah was runner-up to the New York Nets.

"In the last game I ever played at Market Square Arena against the Pacers, I was with Memphis. I had 29 points and we beat 'em." The legend smiled while saying that.

When asked if he still loves the game, Mount responded like the picture-perfect shooter he's always been. "I watch basketball being played today and I'm glad I played in the era I did, because they let shooters shoot then. Now it's kinda slowing it up, passing it eight or 10 times. When we played it was get it up and down, maybe pass not over three times and fire it up. That was a good era for guys that like to score. Now I look at it and I don't think it looks as fun. It's still fun for me to go out and shoot 400 or 500 times a day.

"They took a poll [done by Scripps Howard News Service] two years ago of 30 coaches all over the United States, and I was named the greatest outside shooter that ever lived. Take it or leave it. But I was pretty good. You saw me. Maybe they're talking about me because I'm getting old and they call me a legend now."

Bob Heaton

Clay City High School, Clay City

Year graduated
1975

Major accomplishments
Made the Evansville all-semistate team in 1974; Averaged 17 points as
a senior; Made the all-tournament team in an Indiana State holiday
classic

The "Miracle Man" has never been saluted the way "Larry Legend" and
"Magic" have been for their part in the famous 1979 NCAA
championship game that is considered by many as the contest that
lifted college basketball into the national spotlight. Yet it was Bob Heaton's
second miracle shot of the season that catapulted unbeaten (33-0) and top-
ranked Indiana State and Larry Bird into a monumental showdown with
Michigan State and Ervin "Magic" Johnson.

The right-handed Heaton, playing in his first season at ISU after
transferring from the University of Denver, sank the winning basket with his
left hand as time expired to give the Sycamores a 73-71 victory over
Arkansas and a berth in the Final Four. Had Heaton missed that shot, the
game would have gone into overtime, and perhaps the Bird-Johnson
matchup would never have taken place.

In 1995, Heaton was at the Final Four in Seattle. While there, he and
Billy Packer, veteran CBS college basketball analyst, reminisced about Bob's
second miracle basket and Heaton's roommate that season, Bird. "Packer
made a comment that that shot against Arkansas kinda changed college

basketball a little bit," said Heaton, "because it led to us going to the Final Four and, of course, Larry and Magic getting hooked up. He said, 'Bob, that was a real big basket in looking back.'"

If it hadn't been for the quick reaction of Heaton's grandfather, there might not have been a "Miracle Man." On that wintry day 39 years ago, 11-year-old Heaton was helping store corn on the family farm just outside Cory, Indiana. When he went to pick up an ear that had fallen to the ground, his left shirtsleeve got caught in the corn hiker. His Grandfather turned the machinery off in an instant, but not before Bob suffered a broken bone between his left elbow and shoulder. He was taken to Clay County Hospital in Brazil, where a pin was placed in the arm. It took around 60 stitches to close his wounds. He spent almost two weeks in the hospital and the pin wasn't removed until eight months later.

"It's amazing how God works," said Heaton. "If it wasn't for my grandfather turning off the machinery as fast as he did, there might not have been the left-handed shot that Packer talked about."

Heaton always could shoot well, something he learned while practicing on the 18-foot-by 24-foot, four-inch thick concrete slab his father put down on the farm in November, 1966. "I never will forget the time my older brother John was being recruited by SMU and one of the assistant coaches came up [from Dallas]," said Heaton. "My dad told him about his $100 concrete slab investment, and the coach said, 'Forrest, that's probably going to be the best $100 you ever spent.' John did not go to SMU. As it turned out for me, I had a full-ride scholarship and my folks never had to pay anything."

As a junior at Clay City High, which had 290 students in grades nine through 12, Heaton's basketball team wound up 24-2; losing to Jeffersonville, ranked No. 2 in the state, 52-46 in the semistate at Evansville. "With less than two minutes to go we were up by one," said Heaton, who made the Evansville all-semistate team after logging 19 points and 16 rebounds against the Red Devils. "They were getting ready to shoot a free throw and I looked up, thinking, 'Gosh, we're ahead of these guys. We might beat 'em.' They scored seven straight points and we never scored again. It was truly Hoosier Hysteria back then. We had a lot of people at the game, and they still remember it down home around Clay City."

In Heaton's senior season of 1974-75, he averaged 17 points a game. Clay City was 19-1 during the regular season, but lost to Terre Haute North in the regional final. Although Bob didn't make the Indiana All-Star team,

Denver coach Al Harden, a former Indiana University star from Covington, Indiana, recruited him. He played there two seasons.

Bob probably would have remained at Denver two more years, but the private school became low on funds and decided to drop from Division I to Division II. That prompted Heaton to transfer to ISU. The Sycamores were aware of him because of his outstanding career at Clay City, and the fact he scored 21 points for Denver in a 78-65 loss to ISU in its holiday classic, making the all-tournament team along with Bird.

If there had been a "Sports Center" in 1979, Heaton would have received almost as much airtime as Bird for making his two miracle shots that enabled the Sycamores to nearly complete a perfect season. After making along shot at New Mexico State on February 1 that sent the game into overtime before ISU won, 91-89, he saw himself on ABC national news the next morning in Tulsa, Oklahoma, and he thought, "'Wow, a lot of people just saw what I saw and that was on national TV,' so right then it kinda hit me, like, 'Boy, this is big time.'"

There had been only three seconds left, and ISU trailed, 83-81, when Brad Miley grabbed Greg Webb's missed free throw on a one-and-one free-throw situation. Miley passed to Heaton, who had decided to station himself at mid-court rather than at the Sycamore end of the court following a timeout. He turned and shot.

"I always remember the shot as 52 feet," said Heaton. "As the ball was about halfway there it looked like it was going to go over the backboard. My reaction was, 'Oh, no.' The rest is history. The ball banked in and just then I looked over to my left and here comes Mel Daniels, [former Indiana Pacers center who was an ISU assistant coach at the time]. He gives me a big bear hug. What made that shot so satisfying is that we won the game in overtime [Bird, Carl Nicks and Alex Gilbert had fouled out in regulation]. I remember their fans kept yelling '18 and 1,' with three seconds left, because we were 18-0 at the time."

That shot earned "Miracle Man" his name. Of his second miracle shot, the 6-foot-5 Heaton said, "It happened so darn quick. Of course, we wanted to work the ball to Larry, but he was guarded pretty close by Sydney Moncrief. Steve Reed had an open 18-foot jump shot, but I was a little closer and he passed me the ball. I thought one of the Arkansas players, Scott Hastings, who's like 6-foot-9 or so, was fairly close to me. I was thinking if I go up with my right hand, it might be easier for him to block the shot; but if I come with my left hand and use my body to kinda be between the ball and him, then I might have a chance to score. After I did, people said, 'Well, the Miracle Man again.'"

Heaton, who has been in financial services in Terre Haute since his graduation from ISU in 1980, considers himself one lucky guy to have had a dream season with one of college basketball's most dominant players. "The thing about Larry was the work ethic he exhibited," said Heaton. "I remember the day after the season ended Larry was going to start his student teaching at West Vigo High School and was helping out with the baseball program. By golly, come 7:30 he was up and taking off to do his student teaching.

"You'd think today's college superstars who are going to be the No. 1 NBA draft pick wouldn't be worried about going to do their student teaching. They'd be focusing on what tryouts to go to. Well, to Larry it was a big thing to get that degree, and he had to do his student teaching to get that degree. That was the southern Indiana guy he was, pretty simple, but with the work ethic that it takes."

Bryce Drew

Valparaiso High School, Valparaiso

Year graduated
1994

Major accomplishments
Set a state finals record with 13 assists; Mr. Basketball; Received Trester
Award for mental attitude.

Bryce Drew, who came back home to Indiana in 2005 as an assistant on
his father Homer's Valparaiso University coaching staff after an
outstanding 15-year career, chuckled when he heard the question:
Did you ever dunk?

"In high school I dunked once, against Portage," said Drew. "I had
another one, but it was a half one, so I'm not really going to count it. I didn't
have dunks in college or the pros." The three-point shot was Drew's forte. "I
love the three-point shot," he exclaimed. "That's the greatest rule they ever
put in basketball. In high school I shot a ton of threes, and also in college. I
think when I graduated from college I was sixth all-time on the made list for
three-pointers."

Drew's most famous three-pointer came in the first game of the 1998
NCAA tournament. It is simply referred to as [The Shot] in Valparaiso, and
it gained him instant national notoriety, because ESPN's Sports Center kept
replaying the basket that upset Mississippi, 70-69, as time ran out.

"A lot of people make fun of me by calling it that ('The Shot')," said
Drew. "They play with it a lot, because they played it a lot on TV. We were
down two and we didn't have any timeouts left. We had four seniors on the

floor, so we all knew kinda what to do. We ran our game-ending situation play. And just ran it to perfection."

Jamie Sykes, a pro baseball player who had a strong arm, threw a long pass from out of bounds to one of Valparaiso's 6-6 players, Bill Jenkins. He caught the ball in the air and threw it to Drew.

"When I shot, I thought it was going to be a little short," he said. "I just thank the Lord that it crept over that front rim and went in at the buzzer. All our players were on me after that shot. We all were pretty excited, so we don't remember too much of what was going on."

Drew remembers the shot coming from "25, maybe 24" feet out on the floor at Oklahoma City. Does the shot get longer over time? "It does," he said, laughing. He has a tape of that game at home and can impress his grandkids with it someday.

Valparaiso defeated Florida State, 83-77, in the second round in overtime to advance to the Sweet Sixteen at St. Louis. The Crusaders lost to Rhode Island, 74-68, in the first game. He feels the disappointment from that setback was at least equal to losing to South Bend Clay, 93-88, in overtime in the championship game of the 1994 state tournament. That was the Vikings' only loss in 29 games.

"Yeah, it was pretty disappointing, because it was the same type of situation," said Drew. "We had five seniors on the team, and we feel we didn't play as well in that game as we did the previous one. We were up 10 in the first half, and ended up losing by six. We felt like we could have won if we had played like we did in the first and second rounds. In the next round we would have played Stanford. We had played Stanford earlier in the year, and almost beat them when we weren't playing that well. We thought we had a legitimate chance of going to the Final Four."

Drew says he definitely considers himself a Hoosier even though he was born in Baton Rouge, Louisiana, when his father was an assistant coach on Dale Brown's staff at LSU. He moved with the family to Mishawaka, Indiana, when his son was three years old. Homer Drew became the head coach at Bethel College, an NAIA school in Mishawaka, before moving to the Valparaiso job.

"I come from a basketball family," said Drew. "My mother Janet has seen a ton of games. My older brother Scott went to Butler and played tennis, but he was on dad's staff at Valparaiso before becoming head basketball coach at Baylor. My sister Dana was an Indiana All-Star in 1990, then went to Toledo and became MAC (Mid-America Conference) player of the year twice.

"Dana is married to Casey Shaw, who was drafted by the Philadelphia 76ers and played one season with them. He's played overseas the last eight seasons. They have four kids. Dana used to beat me in basketball until I was a sophomore in high school."

Drew learned the basics of shooting from his father. In the summer, he would tweak his form outdoors. "I looked at pictures of real good shooters, such as Mark Price, Travis Ford, and Steve Kerr," he said. "I looked at how they held their hands and how they held their heads. I tried to emulate that."

It worked. Drew calls his high school senior year a "dream season." He said, "We were 28-0 when we got to the championship game and ranked No. 1 in the state. We had a group of five seniors that had played together for years." Those five were Drew, Tim Bishop, Mark Burnison, Ryan Erdelac, and David Furlin.

"Furlin actually was a junior, but we kinda considered him a senior because we had played together so long," Drew continued. "We were friends on and off the floor and we enjoyed playing together. You know Indiana high school basketball. The whole city got behind us, and we had a tremendous run at the state title."

The Vikings won a classic in the championship game of the Purdue semistate against East Chicago Central. "We were down one, and Tim Bishop hit a shot at the buzzer to give us a one-point victory in four overtimes. Back then there was only one class. I wish they wouldn't have gone to class basketball. I've kinda seen it from both sides. Since I'm coaching at a small college, we'd much rather be in the NCAA tournament, and play against the Dukes and the North Carolinas than to have a smaller tournament with just the smaller Division I schools."

Drew averaged around 25 points as a senior, but he had just nine points in the first game of the state finals at the Hoosier Dome (now the RCA Dome), which Valparaiso won, 84-69, over Indianapolis Ben Davis.

"That was about my lowest scoring game all year," said Drew. "I wasn't really pleased with how I played. I did have 13 assists, and that set the state finals record, so I was doing something good."

South Bend Clay defeated New Albany, 61-57, to advance to the championship game, which the Colonials won, 93-88, in overtime after it was tied, 78-78, in regulation.

"We were up eight with 58 seconds left," said Drew. "To tell you the truth, they made every shot. All we did was we missed one one-and-one and then we had a turnover. Actually, I was the one who turned it over, but if you watch on tape my whole arm got ripped down and they didn't call a foul.

"We made all of our free throws, but they just kept making threes. I think they did a stat that over the fourth quarter and overtime they didn't miss a free throw, and I don't think they missed a three, and they had no turnovers. It obviously was disappointing. I think we were kinda shocked, because we had led for pretty much the whole game and we were in control. I think we still all felt like we were the better team and should have won the game."

During Drew's junior year at Valparaiso U., Bishop, who played in the All-Star series with Drew, was killed in an auto accident while playing professional baseball. "It was very sad," said Drew. "I think most of our team were pallbearers. He's buried only about five minutes from my house."

Houston selected Drew as the 16th pick in the first round of the 1998 NBA draft, because the Rockets had Charles Barkley, and they wanted some three-point shooting to take the pressure off Barkley down low.

"Charles was a great teammate," said Drew. "I think he kinda respected me because I worked so hard." Drew played two years with Houston, one year with Chicago, three years with the Hornets, and one year in Europe, split between Italy and Spain.

Of his pro career, Drew said, "I had a great time and I learned a ton. Some years I played more than others. When I was with Houston we had three of the top 50 [players of all time]: Scottie Pippen, Barkley, and Hakeem Olajuwon. I scored over a thousand points, and I hold the Hornets' record for hitting nine consecutive three-pointers. The good thing was I made the NBA. The average is four years, but I had six, and I felt good about that. I did contribute and had some decent numbers at times.

"My year in Europe was good. I had gotten married, and it was almost like an extended honeymoon for me and my wife, Tara."

Drew believes he could have played a few more years, but with his marriage and the move of his brother to Baylor, he felt the time was right to try coaching, especially with his father.

"My main goal is I want to help my dad win games," said Drew, who chose to play college basketball for his father over Notre Dame. "He's had a great career. I just want to make sure whenever he does decide to retire he goes out a winner." That's the Drew credo.

Carl Erskine

Anderson High School, Anderson

Year graduated
1945

Major accomplishments
As a junior, he was featured in a *Look* magazine article written about
Indiana high school basketball in 1944; Named a Living Legend by The
Indiana Historical Society for his baseball exploits

In his book, *What I learned from Jackie Robinson*, which was published in
March 2005, Carl Erskine of Anderson wrote about how basketball helped
prepare him for his supportive role as a Brooklyn Dodger teammate for
the man who broke Major League Baseball's color barrier.

"What Jackie accomplished was incredible, but I had come from an area
of the country where African Americans lived in my neighborhood," wrote
Erskine. "We went to school together. I had a childhood buddy, Johnny
Wilson, who was African American, and so to me, [big league baseball being
integrated] was life as usual. Life was about people's souls, not their race or
religion or anything else."

Erskine said he learned this lesson early. "[Wilson] and I played together
since grammar school. He and his three brothers and sister were raised by a
single mother. The family was dirt poor but held themselves in high esteem.
He went on to lead his high school team in Indiana to its state championship
in 1946, and he was named Mr. Basketball in Indiana.

"…It was Johnny who taught me to be color-blind, and it was Jackie who
taught me to be 'better,' not bitter, whenever adversity struck. Johnny Wilson

prepared me for Jackie. And Jackie prepared me for my son Jimmy." Jimmy Erskine, born in 1960, has Down syndrome.

Eleven years before Erskine helped pitch the Dodgers to a World Series championship in 1955, he dreamed of winning a state high school basketball title with the Anderson Indians and their superstar center, Wilson, who was Carl's teammate on the Shadeland Elementary School basketball team that had won a city championship in 1939.

"Our 1943-44 Anderson team was rated No. 1 in the state," said the man lovingly referred to as "Oiskin" by the Brooklynese—speaking fans in Ebbets Field. Erskine was one of their Boys of Summer in an outstanding 12-year Dodger career in which he played on six National League pennant-winning teams, won 20 games in 1953, logged two no-hitters, and struck out a record 14 Yankees in a 1953 World Series game.

"Because of that rating, *Look* magazine came out and did a big spread on Indiana high school basketball. They featured the Indians and I still have the article. I was in about three photos."

As the 1944 state tournament approached, Erskine and his teammates, including Wilson, who had been dubbed 'Jumpin' Johnny by the media, were supremely confident.

"We thought we were going to win it all," said Erskine, a 5-foot-9 junior guard who once shot two-handed. "We rolled through the sectional, regional, and semifinals [which is now called semistates]."

As so often happens in sports, the Indians suffered a bad break that shattered their state title dream. Wilson, a sophomore, was undercut on a fast break during the victorious game over Aurora (37-18) in the semifinal round and hurt his back. Anderson did qualify for the state finals by defeating Whiteland, 40-21, but Wilson was not at his best when the Indians traveled to the Indianapolis Coliseum for the final four, which included Evansville Bosse, Kokomo, and LaPorte.

"Butler Fieldhouse [now called Hinkle Fieldhouse] was being remodeled, so the finals were at the Coliseum," said Erskine. "The Coliseum was so strange. The floor was sitting out in the middle of the building, and you didn't have the fans close to the game like in most gyms."

Anderson coach Charles Cummings had Erskine sit next to him during the first game between Bosse and LaPorte. "Bosse had a superstar guard named Broc Jerrel," said Erskine. "I was pretty good defensively and Coach Cummings said, 'You're going to guard Jerrel.' I did watch him, but I didn't get to guard him."

Anderson lost to Kokomo, 30-26, in the second afternoon game before Bosse won its first of two consecutive titles by defeating Kokomo, 39-35, at night.

"None of us played well against Kokomo," said Erskine. "Johnny was stymied by his bad back."

In Erskine's senior year the Indians were beaten in the regional round of the state tournament. "We lost several players from the '44 team, and we didn't have chemistry," he said. Even though Erskine wasn't a prolific scorer, he was offered a chance to play in the Big Ten.

"I never scored more than eight or ten points a game, but I could dribble with either hand, I was a good defensive player, and I loved to pass," said Erskine. "Getting the ball into Johnny was an art in itself. When I was ready to graduate, Coach Cummings said, 'I've got you a scholarship at three places. They're dual scholarships—for basketball and baseball—at Indiana, Purdue, and Ohio State.' It was during World War II and I was 18. Uncle Sam invited me to the Navy."

When Erskine got out of the service, his basketball-playing days were over, but his baseball career continued. His love for the Indians and their famous gym, the Wigwam, never dimmed, though—Carl and his wife, Betty, have had season tickets for Anderson High games for more than 50 years.

"We didn't have anybody come to our Indians baseball games, but for basketball at the Wigwam, they'd pack the place," said Erskine. "I remember coming home after a Dodger season, and someone would stop me on the street and say, 'I remember that game . . .' I thought they meant baseball, but they'd say, 'That game when you made that shot against Kokomo.'

"Getting that Indians uniform was just as much a thrill as getting my first Dodger uniform. I love to go to the Wigwam and walk down the halfways and look at the photos of the teams displayed there."

Erskine had a most unusual introduction to high school baseball. As a 14-year-old freshman, he was called to the office of Archie Chadd, who, at the time, was the football, basketball, and baseball coach. Chadd coached the Indians to state basketball titles in 1935 and 1937.

"I was shaking in my boots," recalled Erskine. "He had seen me play baseball in the park leagues. He said that since I was a mid-year student he wanted me to be with the baseball team as a freshman. I would practice and travel with the team, but I wouldn't play. I had the privilege of being on the baseball team five years. I had never heard of red-shirting."

As a sophomore, Erskine had another unusual athletic experience, this time in basketball under Cummings, who had replaced Chadd.

"He sat us down on the bleachers, took a chalkboard and said, 'I'm going to show you boys a new style of basketball, the fast break, in which you have an outlet pass to a player in the middle of the floor, and two players cut down on either side, and you trap the defense.' Nobody in [the North Central] conference was playing fast-break basketball. Chadd had the old style: slow, deliberate, pass, and cut. Scores started to go up [with the introduction of the fast break] because there was more action and shots."

After retiring from the Dodgers in 1960, Erskine returned to Anderson with Betty and their four children. He has had a successful career in banking, and has enjoyed working with his youngest child, Jimmy, in Special Olympics. Jimmy accompanies his father to the Dodgers fantasy camps in Vero Beach, Florida.

In recent years, Erskine has turned to writing. His first book was entitled *Tales from the Dodgers Dugout*, which is into a second printing. *What I learned from Jackie Robinson* is more of a social account of the parallels Carl saw in the personal struggles that Robinson and Jimmy faced in overcoming racism and the stigma of being handicapped, respectively.

Johnny Wilson

Anderson High School, Anderson

Year graduated
1946

Major accomplishments
Scored a record 30 points for the state championship game in '46;
Mr. Basketball; Named one of Indiana's best 50 players of all time in
1999; Indiana Basketball Hall of Famer.

"Jumpin'" Johnny Wilson, voted Mr. Basketball in 1946 after leading the Anderson Indians to their third state championship, is often asked how he acquired his nickname.

"My sophomore year in high school sports writer Corky Lamm put that on me, 'cause I was the only person dunkin' the ball at that time," said the nearly 6-foot Wilson, who scored 30 points in the Indians' 67-53 victory over Fort Wayne Central in the '46 title game, and broke the previous record of 26 set by Dick Porter of Lebanon in the 1912 championship game.

Wilson can't dunk anymore, but he is still following the bouncing ball. For the last four years, Johnny has been assisting his son, John Jr., who is head coach at Loch Haven (Pennsylvania) State College, an NCAA Division II school.

"I just felt I was too young to give up coaching," said Wilson of his decision to join his son with the Bald Eagles after stints with old Wood High School in Indianapolis (eight years), Malcolm X College in Chicago (20 years), Anderson University (five years), Anderson High boys' team (three years), and Anderson High girls' team (three years). He was head coach at

Wood and Malcolm X, and assistant at the other three stops. "I've been in basketball over 65 years as a player and coach. It's still as exciting as ever. I figure I've got another 12 or 13 years. I'm only 78."

Few relationships in sports have been more enduring and genuine than the one between Wilson and Carl Erskine, a teammate at Anderson High. Wilson went on to play for the Harlem Globetrotters, Erskine to pitch for the Brooklyn Dodgers.

Looking back, Wilson calls his life and career in basketball "tremendous."

"Carl and I talk about it a lot. Here were two kids from the west side of Anderson. He was a little better off then I was, but we were both poor. We were able to fight through it, and make it to the top. He was able to play in the World Series, and I had a chance to travel around the world with the Trotters. Both of us were truly blessed to be able to accomplish that."

The Wilson-Erskine relationship began in grade school, with Erskine jumping center when the pair helped the Shadeland Elementary School team win the city championship in 1939.

"Carl and I started running around together, along with another kid named Jack Rector in about the fourth grade," said Wilson. "We probably spent better than 60 percent of our time together. Jack had a basketball goal on his barn in the alley, and we'd play there day after day, and it'd be ice cold and bloody, whatever. We'd go in and get warm, then go back out and play some more."

Erskine has said that if you could dribble on the frozen mud behind Jack's barn, you could dribble anywhere. "That's right," said Wilson. "I feel we built our skills up by working like that outside all the time. My relationship with Carl, who was a tremendous basketball player, goes on to this day. We play golf together when I'm back in town."

In 1944, the Indians were favored to win the state championship, but Wilson was injured in a semifinal round victory over Aurora. Anderson went on to lose in the afternoon game of the four-team finals, 30-26, to Kokomo.

"We had by far the best team in the state that year," said Wilson. "I went up for a shot against Aurora in the semifinals and a guy undercut me. I landed on my back. I didn't practice before the finals. We beat Kokomo by 13 points on their floor during the regular season. I could rebound in the finals, but I couldn't get going fast enough to get down the floor on the fast break.

"When I left the house that morning, I told my mom to clear off the top of the radio—we didn't have television then—that's where we're gonna put the trophy. It didn't happen."

The Indians did secure the state trophy in 1946, although it didn't appear they would do that well in the tournament after an 11-7 regular season, in which Anderson lost three of its last four games. What turned it around for coach Charles Cummings' crew that had beaten nine teams by an average margin of 15 points in the tournament?

"We had a meeting and Coach tried to find out what was our problem," said Wilson. "One kid said, 'Well, you yell too much.' Cummings took the player into his office, and heard him say that the players wanted to win one game to show people they could win." Wilson said that Cumming's reply was, "We coaches say, 'Don't worry, we're gonna win it all.'

"From that day on we played great ball, and one of the big reasons was Bob Ritter. He and I made the Indiana All-Star team that year. Bob hadn't scored much, but he started wearing glasses. He played better ball every game."

After losing to Fort Wayne Central, 49-22, during the season, many people thought that the Indians had little chance to reverse the score in their title-game rematch. However, Wilson believed otherwise, and scored 30 points on 11 field goals and eight free throws. Ritter had 15 points.

One of Wilson's biggest disappointments came at a banquet following the team's state championship. He wanted to play at Indiana University, but IU coach Branch McCracken squashed that thought during a question-and-answer session.

"McCracken was asked if [I] came to IU, would [I] be able to play basketball," stated Wilson. "Well, at that time no black had ever played for the Big Ten. He said, 'I don't think he could make my team.' He didn't have a single person on that team that I hadn't played against, and I hadn't had any problems."

An all-around athlete, Wilson wound up at Anderson College (now Anderson University), where he played basketball, football, baseball, and ran track. After college Wilson played one year with the Chicago American Giants of the Negro Baseball League as an outfielder.

"There were such names as Elston Howard, Willie Mays, Junior Gilliam, and Joe Black in the league," said Wilson. "I hit around .317. I faced

Joe Black in the Negro World Series. The first time I went to bat against him, I hit a ball almost for a home run. A guy caught it going into the fence. I said, 'Hey, [Black] is mine.' Well, Joe struck me out seven straight times after that. I struck out probably ten times in the regular season."

Of his Mr. Basketball award, Wilson says, "At the time it was the greatest honor I ever had—for a high school kid in Indiana, that is tops. But being rated as one of the 50 best Indiana players ever the night in 1999 when the Pacers opened Conseco Fieldhouse topped Mr. Basketball. People were in there like Oscar [Robertson], the greatest of all time; coach [John] Wooden, Reggie Miller, [Walt] Bellamy, Don Schlundt, Jimmy Rayl, George McGinnis—to be there with names like those was special."

Wilson also says his relationship with his high school coach, Cummings, was "the best. If it hadn't been for him, I don't know where I'd be today. A lot of times you find coaches that when you're through playing you have no more good contact with them. But this guy followed my career all the way.

"After retiring, he moved to Arkansas. When I was coaching at Malcolm X, we played down in Missouri, near Joplin. He drove three different times 100 miles in the winter to watch my team play. That's the kind of man he was."

Bill Shepherd

Hope High School, Hope

Year graduated
1945

Major accomplishments
Indiana All-Star; Indiana Basketball Hall of Famer

Bill and Edie Shepherd have had a love affair with high school sports ever since Bill was a thin 6'1" center on the Hope basketball team in Bartholomew County and Edie was a Red Devil cheerleader. Three years later, when Bill was a junior at Butler University playing for legendary coach Tony Hinkle, he and Edie were married. Their union has produced one of Indiana's most noteworthy legacies.

Three generations of Shepherds have played in the Indiana-Kentucky All-Star series: Bill in 1945; sons Billy and Dave in 1968 and 1970, respectively, when both were named Indiana Mr. Basketball; and grandson Scott, Billy's son, in 1992.

Billy, Dave, and Scott all played for Carmel High School—the first two were coached by their father. Shepherd retired as the Greyhounds basketball coach in 1970, the year Dave scored 40 points in a 76-62 loss to East Chicago Roosevelt in the championship game of the state tournament—a record that still stands for any class.

"I debated whether to get out of coaching," said the elder Shepherd, who coached nine years at Mitchell before moving to Carmel in 1958. "I was only 42 when I quit. We won 337 games all told [against 145 losses], and if I had gone ahead, who knows how many games we would have won.

"But I decided to be the athletic director, a position I held until I retired in 1992. I don't know if it was a good choice or not to quit coaching. You never know. I didn't get to coach my third son, Steve. But it was probably best I leave coaching."

If Shepherd had remained Carmel coach, he might have added another gem to his resume—state champion. Steve was on the 1977 Greyhounds team coached by Eric Clark that won Carmel's only state title. A sophomore guard, Steve scored one point in a 71-60 victory over Columbus East in the afternoon of the state finals at Market Square Arena in Indianapolis. He did not play at night when Carmel defeated East Chicago Washington, 53-52.

Even so, Bill Shepherd had a multitude of thrills as a coach and athletic director. Besides Billy and Dave being voted Mr. Basketball and Steve winning a state championship, Bill saw his Mitchell team win three sectionals, his Carmel teams win the school's first sectional in 41 years in 1965 and four more, his 1968-69 team have an unbeaten regular season, his 1970 team win the school's first regional and semistate titles, and his teams finish his coaching career with 50 victories at home without a defeat.

"It has been a great ride," said Shepherd, whose greatest personal honor occurred in 1975 when he was named to the Indiana Basketball Hall of Fame. Bill and Billy went into the Butler Hall of Fame together in 2001.

Bill and Edie estimate they have attended well over 10,000 high school sporting events for their four children and 15 grandchildren. "We're probably a little different than most grandparents or parents, in the fact that we love sports," said Bill. "When the kids are involved, we don't care where it is."

The Shepherds have toured the country to see Billy play for the Butler Bulldogs, Virginia, San Diego, and Memphis in the old American Basketball Association; Dave play for Indiana, and Mississippi; Steve play for Indiana Central (now the University of Indianapolis); Scott play for Florida State; and Billy's son Jeff for Huntington College. They also have journeyed east and west to watch daughter Cindy McCurdy's two sons play basketball at Southern Connecticut and Arkansas. In addition, Bill and Edie have seen Stacia, Steve's daughter, play basketball for Carmel; and Carly, Billy's daughter, play golf for the Greyhounds.

The Shepherds' odyssey began humbly in Hope, which had only 17 students in Bill's graduating class. "Our offense was kind of unique," he said.

"It was built around getting the ball into me, and individually playing one-on-one."

Unique or not, the offense worked. Hope defeated Morristown, 16-14, in its final game at home in 1945 to finish the regular season 19-1. "Our gym seated about 1,200 and they turned 'em away, the only time it happened," Shepherd recalled. "I got 12 of our 16 points. It wasn't that we were holding the ball or they were holding the ball, it's just amazing how the game has changed."

In the sectional at Shelbyville, Hope beat Clifford, Waldron, Shelbyville, and Morristown. The Red Devils defeated Greensburg and Franklin in the regional at Shelbyville to advance to the semifinals at Butler Fieldhouse (now Hinkle Fieldhouse). Hope lost to Indianapolis Broad Ripple in the afternoon, 54-36.

Shepherd chuckles when he remembers that game. "Phil Eskew Sr., who later became Indiana High School Athletic Association commissioner, made some bad calls as one of the officials," he said. "On the way out Edie, who was on the floor as one of our cheerleaders, gave him a little problem. He never forgot it. But we became good friends. Phil remembered Edie when he was commissioner and encouraged me to run for the IHSAA board."

Asked if he would have preferred playing in class basketball with the chance of winning a state title, Shepherd replied with an emphatic no. "I would rather have gone to the semifinals in one-class basketball [as Hope did in '45] than win a state title in class basketball."

Although Bill wound up at Indiana University as a freshman, he thought he would go to Butler in the fall of 1945, because his father, who was in the military service at the time, knew several people associated with Hinkle. "My dad was an avid basketball fan, and always wanted me to be a coach and get an education he never got," Shepherd said. "He took me to all the high school state tournaments. We used to go to the old Claypool Hotel in Indianapolis where they would scalp tickets. We'd buy some, because Hope didn't get many.

"Dad knew Hinkle was a pretty good coach. I probably would have fit in their pattern much better than I would have at IU, because I didn't have a lot of speed. I was an offensive player in high school, and in college I wasn't big enough to play in the pivot. At 6'1", I had to move to forward."

Harry Goode, who was the IU coach while Branch McCracken was in the service, talked Shepherd into enrolling at Bloomington. He made the team, but decided to transfer to Butler after one season because he didn't think he'd fit in the "Hurryin' Hoosier" offense when McCracken returned from service.

"I'll tell you what convinced me about Hinkle," said Shepherd. "IU played at Butler that year. I got to dress for all home games, and made about five or six road trips with the varsity. I didn't get to play a lot, but it was good experience for me. I watched Butler work the ball, and I had never seen anything like it. How they'd pass the ball and cut through, and all at once somebody would go up for a nice shot 15, 20 or 25 feet away.

"In my three years at Butler, we ended up beating both IU and Purdue three times. The amazing thing is I played some of my best games against Indiana. I didn't start at Butler the first two years. The last year Hinkle would start Charlie Maas, but after the first five or six minutes I would see Hinkle's assistant, Bob Dietz, punch Tony to get me in the game, and I'd play the rest of the way most of the time. Any success I had as a coach, I give that success to Mr. Hinkle."

Billy Shepherd

Carmel High School, Carmel

Year graduated
1968

Major accomplishments
Still holds six Carmel scoring records, including most career points (2,465) and most points in a game (70); Mr. Basketball; Indiana Basketball Hall of Famer.

Billy Shepherd of Carmel had a remarkable and rewarding career. The Indiana Mr. Basketball turned down a chance to play for fabled coach John Wooden at UCLA in order to accept a scholarship from legendary Butler University coach Tony Hinkle. Hinkle's winning recruiting message was that the Bulldogs just happened to have a pair of size nine basketball shoes—Shepherd's size.

It happened this way for the eldest son of Bill Shepherd, who not only was an Indiana All-Star himself in 1945, but also had two sons who became Indiana All-Stars—Billy in 1968 and David in 1970, who was also voted Indiana Mr. Basketball that year—as well as a grandson, Scott, in 1992.

In the fall of 1967, Bill Shepherd, who at the time was the basketball coach Carmel, invited his son, Billy, to a Greyhound football game. Hinkle was the high school football official assigned to the Carmel game. Bill Shepherd wanted his son to meet his college basketball coach.

"I had met Coach Hinkle a number of times, because I grew up going to Butler games," said Shepherd. "Here's what was funny. He said, 'Kid, what size shoe do you wear, anyway?' I said, 'Oh, I think size nine.' He said, 'That's great.

We've got that size out there at Butler.' That was his way of saying he wanted me to come to Butler. That's the way Mr. Hinkle was, it was either kid or Carmel or that type of thing."

Shepherd, who says he could have gone to any school in the country, chose Butler over UCLA for three reasons: (1) he wanted to stay close enough to home so his parents could see him play; (2) he wanted to play in a city (Indianapolis) with an ABA team (the Indiana Pacers were an original ABA franchise in 1967), because one of the best parts of Shepherd's game was his shooting range—he figured if he was ever going to be able to play pro ball, it was in the ABA, which was the only place at the time that used the three-point shot, and (3) he thought his dad might have a chance to get the job at Butler when Hinkle retired.

"I knew that question would come up at the end of my sophomore year at Butler, because Hinkle was going to turn 65," said Shepherd. However, Bill Shepherd did not succeed Hinkle.

Shepherd laughs when he recalls the time his son, Scott, and some of his cousins had lunch with Wooden.

"Scott was working in Los Angeles," said Shepherd. "I told my kids years later that Coach Wooden did not recruit Henry Bibby until after I called him and told him I wasn't coming to UCLA. My dad had kept a relationship with Coach Wooden over the years. Wooden showed Scott and the cousins his memorabilia, which was a neat deal for all those grandchildren of grandpa Shepherd.

"When Scott was getting ready to leave, he said, 'Oh, by the way, Coach, I've got to ask you a question. My dad always told me you did not recruit Henry Bibby until he called you and said he wasn't coming to UCLA.' Coach Wooden put his hand on Scott's shoulder and said, 'Scott, just let your dad believe what he wants to.' He didn't verify it. I guess it was his way of saying he had other things in the works. Yeah, UCLA was hot and heavy after me."

Shepherd could always score. He still holds six individual Carmel records: most points for a career, 2,465 (1964-68); most points for a game, 70 (against Brownsburg on January 6, 1968); most field goals in a game (31 vs. Brownsburg in '68); most field goals in a career, 917; most free throws made in a career, 631; and best free-throw percentage in a season, .840 (1966-67).

For his three-year career at Butler (freshmen weren't eligible in the 1968-69 season), Shepherd set five individual scoring records that still stand: best scoring average for a season, 27.8 (1969-70); best career average, 24.1 (1969-

72); most points as a sophomore, 724 (1969-70); most field goal attempts for a game, 36 (vs. Indiana State, January 7 and February 7, 1970); and most field goal attempts for a career, 652 (1969-72). He also is the Bulldogs' fifth-leading all-time scorer with 1,733 points,

Did Shepherd's arm ever get tired from taking so many shots? "Heck no," he said. "In high school that was normal. I shouldn't say normal. But on any given night I was capable of getting up 30 shots. It was a little bit of a different era back then. It was the era of the Mounts, the Maraviches, the Murphys, the Issels, who scored a lot of points."

Shepherd's most memorable Butler game came on February 23, 1970. It was Hinkle's farewell appearance at the fieldhouse named after him.

"They were standing six deep, up above and down below," said Shepherd. "There were probably 17,000 fans in a place that held 15,000 (capacity is now 11,043). We played Notre Dame that game and Austin Carr was on that team. He had 50 and I had 38. I might have had 50 if they had the three-point line. They beat us, 121-114.

"You don't realize at the time all the emotion that runs through something like that night. But it being Coach Hinkle's last game, it was a special occasion. Those four years at Butler were great. You meet lifelong friends in college, and having the opportunity to play for Coach Hinkle, and play on his last team, was something I'll never forget."

Shepherd played three years in the ABA after leaving Butler. While on the Virginia Squires he played with Julius Erving and George Gervin. He played point guard for the San Diego Conquistadores and coach Wilt Chamberlain. When Shepherd was on the Memphis Tams, his teammates included former Pacers Roger Brown, Mel Daniels, Rick Mount, and Tom Owens.

Shepherd chuckled while recalling his season with the Squires. "I was our 20-point man," he said. "I got in when we were 20 ahead or 20 behind. But what it taught me was respect for a lot of teammates I'd played with in the past. Now all of a sudden I'm sitting on the bench supporting players that are playing the game, and that made me realize some of the good relationships I had with kids over a period of years that maybe didn't get the minutes, yet still remained my friends in high school and college."

After being released by the Squires, Shepherd tried out with the Conquistadores and made the team, which surprised him because Chamberlain became the coach a week before the season was to begin.

"I said, 'Man, I'm 5-10 and Chamberlain is 7-1 or 7-2; he's not going to like me,'" Shepherd recalls. "But we had a big scrimmage in Chamberlain's second practice. My passing and ball handling were really shining that day. Chamberlain called me and said, 'Hey, Shepherd, I want you to know I really like your game. You're going to be a part of this team this season.' Knowing the coach had confidence in me set me up for a much better season as a starter."

Shepherd, who calls himself a journeyman player, took a job with Converse following his three-year pro stint and remained with the company eight years. After he left, he started his own business, Billy Shepherd SPORTS (Speaking Publicly On Raising Talented Student-Athletes). He also writes a weekly column that helps parents with issues concerning conflicts with their kids' athletics. It appears in several newspapers around the country. In addition, Shepherd has a high school basketball publication and a recruiting Web site aimed at helping kids figure out where they might want to go to college. Shepherd put his AAU coaching experience to good use during the 2003-2004 high school season when he coached Muncie Central to a 20-4 record after the late Bill Harrell was dismissed. Shepherd was not retained by the Bearcats, but that didn't keep him from his favorite sport. "Billy the Kid" visits close to 100 college, high school, and junior high basketball games every season.

Dave Shepherd

Carmel High School, Carmel

Year graduated
1970

Major accomplishments
Holds two state high school records—40 points for a state championship
game as a senior and 1,079 points for a season as a senior (1969-70); Mr.
Basketball; Indiana Basketball Hall of Famer

A s Dave Shepherd sat in his memorabilia office at his award-winning
insurance agency in Carmel, he smiled far more than he frowned
while recalling the highs and lows of his high school and college
basketball careers. Shepherd not only holds two coveted Indiana high school
scoring records, he might possibly hold the record for amount of
associations to Indiana trivia questions.

"There have been three Mr. Basketballs born in Bedford's Memorial
Hospital," said Shepherd, who scored 40 points in Carmel's 76-62 loss to
East Chicago Roosevelt in the title game of the 1970 state high school
tournament, and finished the season with 1,079 points—both totals being
records. "Who were they? Billy Shepherd, Dave Shepherd, and Damon
Bailey."

Billy, Shepherd's older brother, was Carmel's first Mr. Basketball in
1968. Shepherd was the second in 1970. His father, Bill, who retired as the
Carmel coach after the Greyhounds lost in the '70 title game, was coach at
Mitchell when his sons were born in nearby Bedford. Bailey was Mr.
Basketball in 1990 when he led Bedford North Lawrence to the state
championship.

Chuckling, Shepherd says he also is a trivia question nationally. "They have a trivia question every once in a while in the *Chicago Tribune*. They'll list the 40 or 50 players who left Indiana University while Bobby Knight was coach, and they'll want to know who was the first to leave. The first is Dave Shepherd. It's something I've had to live with, but it's worked out."

Shepherd, who transferred to the University of Mississippi where he became all-Southeastern Conference and Academic All-American as a senior, can chart his success in the two awards his insurance agency has recently received. In 2003, the Independent Insurance Agents of Indiana named his business "Agency of the Year." A year later, the agency received an honorable mention in the National Underwriter's "Commercial Insurance Agency of the Year" award program.

Of the 2004 award, which reflects the concepts of teamwork he absorbed at Carmel High, IU and Mississippi, Shepherd says, "That's the Heisman of our industry. We run the agency like a sports team. You've gotta have student managers, coaches, great players and role players. We hire people for certain positions just like you'd fill out a sports organization. Everybody can't be a leading scorer."

Shepherd's oldest child, daughter Kelly Shepherd Kakone, has been with the insurance company a little over a decade, and has been president for five years. None of his four children (second wife Sally has three children) played high school basketball at Carmel.

Shepherd almost followed his brother, Billy, to Butler University after becoming the state's 11th all-time leading high school career scorer with 2,226 points for three seasons (Billy is fifth with 2,465 for four seasons). Shepherd says he would have become a Bulldog if his father had gotten the Butler coaching job following Tony Hinkle's retirement in 1970. Bill Shepherd did not get the job, so Shepherd opted to attend IU and play for coach Lou Watson.

Shepherd's IU career began brilliantly. In his first season as a Hoosier (freshmen weren't eligible for varsity competition then), he averaged 26 points, with a high of 44 against Ball State—a freshman record. At the end of the 1970-71 season, Watson was fired as IU coach and succeeded by Knight.

Heading into the 1971-72 season, Shepherd was upbeat and thinking he would be "Bobby's boy, so to speak." But on the first day of practice in October after Assembly Hall had just opened, life changed suddenly for Shepherd.

On the way home to attend Carmel's homecoming football game following basketball practice, the car in which he was riding with several other students was hit head-on by a drunk driver. Shepherd suffered a broken ankle, a broken jaw, and rib injuries. He had more than 100 stitches in his face and his jaw was wired shut, which caused him to lose 20 pounds and quite a bit of strength before returning to practice in January.

"I actually worked myself back into the starting lineup, and things then went to hell in a hand basket," lamented Shepherd. "My first game back we had a one-point lead and the ball out of bounds with three seconds to go against Wisconsin, but lost in overtime. I probably should have red-shirted, but we were really short-handed. We only had eight scholarship players, and [Knight] wanted me to get back, but I just couldn't. Before that accident there's no question I was going to be the point guard, and I was going to be there forever. But after I got injured I never was the same player."

Shepherd says he learned more about basketball from his dad than anybody, but admits Knight had a lot of positive influence on him. "Everybody looking back thinks that Bobby Knight is all bad," he explained. "He isn't. The discipline you learn from him, there's a lot of good there. And there were a lot of things from a team standpoint I learned in my year under him."

Shepherd says he didn't leave IU and Knight on the best of terms, but he believes the good Knight did for the program—all the national championships, all the Big Ten titles, the team concept, the graduation rate of his players, and the discipline—far outweighed the bad.

"It's just a shame," Shepherd emphasized. "The way Knight went out as the Hoosier coach."

Seeking a new environment and conference, Shepherd left liberal IU to attend a conservative school in Oxford, Mississippi, in the fall of 1972. "It gave me a chance to get back physically," he said of the year he had to sit out.

Shepherd was second in the SEC in scoring his senior year with a 21-point average, and was the Rebels' MVP. "Things couldn't have gone better at Ole Miss," he said.

Shepherd has never let life's foils dim his optimism. He was, naturally, disappointed when the Carmel school board passed a ruling just before he was to enter high school that freshmen would not be eligible for varsity competition.

"I wasn't happy with the ruling, but it wasn't the end of the world," said Shepherd. "I'm one of those guys who believes everything happens for a reason. I figure if I get upset about things, you can't change it anyway. Just try to look at the other side of it, and say something good will happen. And it usually does."

Many good things happened to Shepherd at Carmel High. He never lost a home game in his three seasons, going 50-0, and as a junior he led the Greyhounds to their only undefeated regular season (20-0). They lost to Marion in the final game of the regional to finish 24-1. As a senior, Shepherd averaged 37.2, with a high game of 66 and a low game of 24.

With the help of Dr. Tom Brady of Indianapolis, Shepherd gutted his way into the final game of the 1970 state tournament in which he hit 14 of 39 shots from the floor, and 12 of 14 free throws to break Oscar Robertson's record of 39 points, set in 1956 when Indianapolis Crispus Attucks became the first unbeaten state champion.

Early in the first game against Highland in the Anderson regional, Shepherd was hit in his right knee so bad "they had to split my pants up the side just so I could get them off" when Dr. Brady arrived at the team's hotel in late afternoon. Dr. Brady drained the knee, and Shepherd wound up with 88 points in two victories that day.

Shepherd's pain continued in the semistate and finals, but he persevered and scored 125 points in those last four games. Asked how he felt getting ready to play East Chicago Roosevelt, Shepherd said, "Bad. But that's one game I can say if we would have played it 100 times, we would have lost 98. They were like a college team. There is no team with our talent that could ever have gotten as far as we got."

Being Mr. Basketball grows more precious with each passing year, says Shepherd, who vows he would not have wanted to play in a class basketball atmosphere. "In the back of your mind you know it's there, [Mr. Basketball], and it's something you want to do," he stated. "But you don't realize what you've done until you're out. It's something when you get some age on you—I'm in my 50s now—and people still remember. It kinda makes you feel good."

Hallie Bryant

Attucks High School, Indianapolis

Year graduated
1953

Major accomplishments
Mr. Basketball; Named "Star of Stars" in the Indiana-Kentucky All-Star series; Indiana Basketball Hall of Famer

Basketball has taken Hallie Bryant to heights he had never thought possible while a youth in Calhoun Falls, South Carolina, which he calls a "little resort."

"I had some friends who say they tried to get me to play basketball," said Bryant, who, according to his resume on the Indiana Basketball Hall of Fame Web site, helped lay the foundation for greatness at Indianapolis Crispus Attucks High School in the early 1950s.

"I saw some of it, but it wasn't something that was high on my list. They were playing ball, really it was dust bowl, but football was intriguing to me because you could throw a bullet. I was into hunting and fishing and doing all the things country boys do."

All of that changed one day as Bryant sat in art class at Public School 24. The 1983 hall of fame inductee and Indiana's Mr. Basketball in 1953 said that, "There was a playground just a few feet from the window of the art class. For some reason they allowed those kids to play basketball out there. They were having so much fun and that was distracting me, but I liked that and I couldn't wait 'til I got out of school. That's where I first started getting interested in basketball. And I watched the people who did it well. I went from there to Public School 17 where I met coach Ray Crowe."

It was the late Ray Crowe, who led all-black Attucks High School to successive state championships in 1955 and '56 with Oscar Robertson as the catalyst, who inspired Bryant to become more than he ever dreamed he could be.

"Ray Crowe was such a dignified person, like a movie star," said Bryant. "Kids looked up to him because of the way he carried himself, his character, his demeanor. He was a no-foolishness type guy. He just so matched my father's total demeanor. Of course my dad was not formally educated, but I thought he was brilliant, because he had good common sense. Ray Crowe was singing the same song, so to speak, as far as character, so we blended quite well."

Bryant's family prepared him well for life in all-black schools before civil rights took root in this country.

"My great grandmother, my grandparents and my father would always stress that we were not better than anyone and not less than anyone," he said. "That has served as my foundation. Maybe they knew we would run into some bigotry, run into some negative things, not just by whites but people period. Your own people can give you bigotry, too, and ignorance.

"So I don't have the anger and get disturbed when someone says something or treats me some way. I guess you can call it self-image, self-esteem, as you've learned how to use the language a little bit. That was the one thing in particular that was ingrained in me, so the anger wasn't there. I love people. I didn't know how to express it at one time. I like to think I have learned a little how to do it."

Bryant says his days at Attucks provided a super experience to grow, to get to know oneself better, and know other people better. "Anyone who misses that, whether you're at an all-black school or integrated school, those are the learning years, those are the growing years, those are the years you pick up the tools that help you to negotiate through life on all levels."

When he was nine, Bryant's family moved to Indianapolis from South Carolina seeking more opportunities. "The teachers were kind," he said. "The schools in Indianapolis were segregated, also, but there wasn't anything that was demeaning about it. They took interest in you, because the good teachers knew that you would get out in the world and have to compete. So they tried to teach you something other than what was in the books. They taught you manners, they taught you to be on time. They taught you the basic things that they thought you might have missed in the homes."

And Ray Crowe was teaching Bryant and his fellow basketball players, Willie Gardner, Bailey Robertson, Oscar's older brother, and Bob Jewell, how to play the game right. Bryant couldn't play varsity as a freshman. "It wasn't a written rule," he said, "but I guess a lot of people thought you should play reserve the first year. We would beat the varsity in practices. But for some reason there was that old mind-set, 'Let these guys get whatever they need in order to play varsity.' Now kids can play as freshmen."

In 1951, when Bryant was a sophomore, Attucks went to the state tournament finals at Butler Fieldhouse (now Hinkle Fieldhouse). The Tigers lost to Evansville Reitz, 66-59, in the afternoon with Gardner scoring 22 points, Bryant ten, Jewell six, and Robertson two. Jewell was named recipient of the Trester Award for mental attitude after Muncie Central defeated Reitz, 60-58, in the championship game.

"That state finals was a great experience," said Bryant, "but losing wasn't something that I took to very well. If you don't hurt a little, you don't grow. But I think I overdid that. I learned from the hurt."

As a junior, Bryant's Attucks team lost to Tech in the Indianapolis sectional, 63-60. Tech went on to become runner-up to Muncie Central in the state championship game. In 1953 Attucks lost to Shelbyville in the Indianapolis semifinals (now semistate), 46-44.

"Losing any game hurts," said Bryant. "But when you lose in the tournament it hurts even more. But again, that which will not kill you will make you grow."

The Mr. Basketball title salved Bryant's hurt of losing in the state tournament. "You dream of being Mr. Basketball from the time you're in grade school. It's like winning the Heisman Trophy. In this state that's the epitome of success. Winning that was for your community, and all the people who loved you, and the people who suffered with you."

After being named "Star of Stars" in the Indiana-Kentucky All-Star series of 1953, Bryant went to Michigan and Michigan State on recruiting visits. But people kept telling him to stay close to home for his college basketball, so he opted for IU, where he again got into a growth situation.

"I had a lot of hurtin' as far as not living up to my expectations," he said. "I don't want to get into why, because I'm sure I had a lot to do with that, too. But overall it was a great learning experience."

In 1957, Bryant's senior season in which he was a co-captain, IU was co-Big Ten champion with Michigan State. At that time the NCAA allowed only one team from a conference to go to the national tournament. Since IU had been to the tournament before, Michigan State was invited. The Hoosiers stayed home.

Bryant was drafted by the St. Louis Hawks of the NBA. "I don't like to talk about race, but you have to stop and think about it. There had only been about three black players in the NBA at that time. St. Louis had never had one. I was drafted along with one or two other black players. I played in all the preliminary games, and was averaging about 16, 17 points. I can remember the coach, Alex Hannum, talking about a young man, Wilfong I believe was his name. He went to Missouri. 'You came so close to making it and you deserve to make it, but we have to go with the local kid.' It probably turned out to be the best thing."

The Hawks called Abe Saperstein, founder and owner of the Globetrotters. Willie Gardner had played with the Globetrotters, and he told Bryant all about them. "Willie had paved the way with the Trotters, and they said Bryant played with Willie Gardner, he may be okay." Bryant went to the Trotters after he had joined the Army and spent two years in service as a lieutenant.

The Globetrotters opened Bryant's eyes to a whole different world. "I learned the Globetrotters are not just here in the United States," he said. "They go all over the world [I visited 87 countries with them]. And man, Saperstein took a liking to me. He saw I was a pretty nice kid, because I didn't do a lot of talking. He probably thought I had some sense. It's good to have manners and be polite. Once you carry yourself in a respectful way people bend over backwards for you, in most cases.

"My skills had to play a big part, too. But all of that plays a part when you're with an organization; whether it's basketball or any type business you work for. That harmony thing I talk about in my book, and when you're trying and being honest, and people can trust you, which enhances your opportunity in every area of life. You learn this in athletics."

While playing 13 full seasons with the Trotters and then taking on public relations duties, Bryant formulated his own one-man show. Instead of just talking about the Trotters, he would demonstrate some of the ball-handling skills they were renowned for.

"I like to think of myself as an 'edutainer'—[teacher and entertainer],"
he said. "Teach people with humor and that breaks down the barrier."

For years now, Bryant has been delivering seminars "that will help
anyone who desires to have a winning edge in life," it says in his book that
was co-authored by O'Merrial Butchee, CEO of Visionamics of Munster,
Indiana, and edited by Bill Shover, former director of the Indiana All-Stars
as an executive at the Indianapolis Star.

In addition to being an "edutainer" for many major companies, Bryant
is now "enjoying doing seminars in the Indianapolis Public Schools. I'm at
my best when I let my heart talk. Basketball is a fun game, life is a fun game.
Basketball teaches you how to win, how to lose, how to get along with
people."

Bryant and his life partner, Deloris Hayes, have two daughters. "Deloris
has allowed me to be fully who I am—a free spirit," he said. "I thank God
for her."

Mike Warren

South Bend Central High School, South Bend

Year graduated
1964

Major accomplishments
Held an Elkhart regional-record 43 points as a senior; Graduated
from Central as Bears' career, season, and single-game scoring leader
South Bend Hall of Famer; Indiana Basketball Hall of Famer

As Mike Warren sat in church not long ago, the sermon themed "Do We Really Deserve God's Love?" made a big impression on the former South Bend Central High School standout guard who went on to help Hoosier legend John Wooden land his third and fourth NCAA Division I national championships.

Those words in the sermon got Warren, who now lives in Woodland Hills, California, to thinking "about what we want and what we're given. I came up with, 'I don't have all that I want, but I have more than I deserve.'"

Warren doesn't have a state high school tournament championship because Muncie Central beat his South Bend Central team, 65-61, in the 1963 title game. And he didn't get the spot on the 1964 Indiana All-Star team that he unequivocally believes he earned. However, he did earn a starting spot for three years at UCLA, an All-American status with the Bruins, and was called "the smartest player he ever coached" by Wooden. In addition, he received an Emmy nomination for his performances in the television series Hill Street Blues in 1983, and the NAACP's Image Award as best actor the same year.

"Coach Wooden said having me on the floor was like having a coach out on the floor," said Warren, "and I had the rare privilege of being captain two years in a row. A large part of that was that there were no seniors when I was a junior."

That was the 1966-67 season when Lew Alcindor (now Kareem Abdul-Jabbar), Lucius Allen, Lynn Shackelford, and Kenny Heitz, all sophomores, joined Warren in the starting lineup. The young lineup helped UCLA defeat Houston, 73-58, and Dayton, 79-64, to win the NCAA Division I championship in Louisville, Kentucky. The Bruins finished 30-0.

When Warren was a senior, UCLA met Houston on January 20, 1968, before a record crowd for a college basketball game—52,693—in the Houston Astrodome. UCLA was ranked No. 1, Houston No. 2. Houston won, 71-69. The Bruins avenged the loss by beating Houston, 101-69, in the semifinals of the NCAA Final Four at the Los Angeles Sports Arena. They then went on to defeat North Carolina, 78-55, for the national title.

It was almost predestined that Warren would wind up at UCLA. His father, a janitor at the South Bend Tribune, moved his family from a predominantly black area on the south side of the city to a predominantly white area on the north side when Warren was young.

"My father envisioned a better life for [my brother and sister and myself] in terms of education," Warren said.

The elementary and junior high schools in the Warrens' new neighborhood fed into South Bend Central, where Wooden coached from 1934 to 1943. This is where Warren was influenced by three coaches who made a lasting impression—Paul Sloan, Don Koz, and Jim Powers.

"Paul Sloan was a wonderful gentleman who I think probably saw promise in me as a basketball player, maybe even before my parents did," said Warren. Sloan started the third grader on the sixth grade team.

Koz, who coached Warren in junior high school, had played for Wooden in high school. Warren says that he was much like his UCLA mentor. "[Koz] taught English and quoted poetry. He was a disciplinarian and a fundamentalist in regard to basketball. Sloan and Koz not only talked to me about basketball, but about education; and whenever you play you play your hardest, you're not just playing for yourself or for your school, you represent your family."

Warren says South Bend Central, which was phased out in 1970, was "one of the elite schools in the state of Indiana, at least in terms of combining academics with athletics. Some of the guys I looked up to as a youngster played on championship teams at Central, and when I transferred there I played for a guy who's still one of my dear friends." That "dear friend" is Jim Powers.

Warren continued, "Not unlike Don Koz, he had been a high school and a college player for John Wooden [at Indiana State]. I don't think it was any mistake that I had become pretty proficient in the fundamentals of basketball. The foundation was laid early by Paul Sloan, and it was built upon by Don Koz, and even more so by Jim Powers."

In the 1962-63 regular season, Powers' Bears dealt Muncie Central its only loss, winning 71-66, at Muncie's home. "The fans were very rabid, but they loved their Bearcats," said Warren. "It was probably one of the loudest places we ever played in.

"We played them again in the state finals. I played on two national championship teams at UCLA, and to this day if someone were to ask, 'Would you give back one of those championships for an Indiana state high school championship?' I would not hesitate, I would say, 'absolutely.'" Warren, who scored 22 points in the title game, remembers being on the runner-up stand and crying his eyes out.

After losing to Elkhart in the regional as a senior, Warren, who was only the second player ever to make Central's varsity as a freshman, was not chosen for the Indiana All-Star team.

"Myself and Vernon Payne, who played at Michigan City [and at Indiana University]—I think we were without question two of the best guards in the state," said Warren. "It was ironic. We both made all-state, but neither one of us was picked for the All-Star team. I was devastated. I had played against some of those guys who made the team, and I had outplayed them. I could not understand how I could be overlooked. There was some talk about it being racial [because all 10 of the All-Stars selected were white], and some talk about it being a regional thing.

"To make that team was always a dream. I can't say it was ever a goal. But I was naïve and thought that if you played well, and had the respect of people you played against, that the whole idea of selecting players would be a fair process. That taught me that it was not a fair process. Probably the most disappointing thing about the whole matter was that for the first time I saw where politics played a very important part in the game of basketball."

Warren approached his basketball future with an open mind. He visited Kansas and had a trip to Michigan scheduled. But a friend of Wooden's, Walt Kindy, asked Warren if he would be interested in visiting UCLA. He had an aunt and uncle living in California that he adored, so he jumped at the opportunity to see them and Wooden.

There was snow on the ground in South Bend, and it was bitterly cold when Warren flew west. As he walked from the plane to the terminal in Los Angeles, Warren was exhilarated by the warm air that hit him in the face. He then rode with UCLA assistant coach Jerry Norman on a freeway—"there are no freeways in South Bend," Warren remembers thinking—to the UCLA campus.

"I was mesmerized by the beauty of it all," said Warren. "I remember seeing an orange tree. My experience was that oranges came in crates." His first impression upon meeting Wooden was that he was "like a soft shoe sales person, not one of those guys when you come in the store says, 'Can I show you some shoes right away, a great pair?' He didn't do any of that stuff. Coaches on some of my other visits said I was going to start as a sophomore—you couldn't start as a freshman then—and that I would have this and that. It was not disappointing, it was just different. He took out a set of plans for a new arena and said as a sophomore 'this is where you would play.' He didn't say I would start."

Wooden obviously had been told by Powers and Kindy that Warren could play for UCLA, "but no one knows how well you're going to do in college until you get there. I was 5'10" and barely weighed 155 pounds. Wooden was really warm and cordial, and I liked him. But I must say it was probably more the weather, and the fact my aunt and uncle lived in California than anything."

Warren told Powers upon his return to South Bend that the visit went well, but he added, "'I can't say whether [Wooden] really wanted me or I couldn't get in. I'll go to USC Cal-State. I jut want to go to California.' Powers said, 'If you don't play for Johnny Wooden in California, you're not going to go to California.'"

In Warren's mind, he thought going so far away from home would allow him to be his own man. "Little did I know that running into John Wooden was like running into my father's brother," he said. "They had the same kind of principles and morals, and trying to get out from under that, I ran smack-dab into it."

What was it like playing for Wooden? "Have you ever ridden in a Bentley or a Rolls Royce?" said Warren. "I never have, but I played for John Wooden, and I would imagine that's what it would be like. As an 18-, 19-, 20-, 21-year-old, you don't really get that close to the head coach, at least we didn't. There seemed to be a kind of—not a barrier—but we were closer to the assistant coaches. I wouldn't say Jerry Norman was any more accessible, but Wooden was like a god. He was an authority figure.

"But for about the last 15 years I have forged a relationship with him that is truly unique and special to me. I see him as a man, and I know the man a lot better now than I did as an 18-year-old. I now respect his wisdom and intelligence, where as an 18-year-old I couldn't possibly know."

After graduating from UCLA, Warren was drafted by Seattle of the NBA. He received a contract offer that he thought seemed like junk mail addressed to occupant. "It was never a dream growing up to play professional sports because there was always a bias against the little guy," he said. Warren would have had to try out, and in his estimation, the contract was so bad that he decided to go in a different direction.

Warren, a television major at UCLA, says his experience with the Bruins prepared him to be on a show like Hill Street, and that playing with Kareem Abdul-Jabbar, who in Warren's opinion is still the greatest college basketball player ever, taught him that the spotlight is pretty broad.

"Though you may not be the focal point, all the time in that spotlight—even if you're in the fringes—that's pretty cool, too," said Warren. "So on Hill Street, I again was working in an environment where it was a team, I thought. The writers gave us all wonderful things to do, not all the time, but some of the time. I was young in my career and I was working with really qualified, talented people that I learned from. It was as special as the UCLA experience."

Warren is still acting and producing. "But my focus is on my family," he said. He and second wife Jenny have two young children. He also has two adult children by his first wife, and two grand- children.

Of his relationship with Wooden, Warren says, "For me to come into his life, and for him to come into mine—I'm more fortunate than he, to say the least. I'm a huge fan of his and will love him forever."

Harley Andrews

Terre Haute Gerstmeyer High School, Terre Haute

Year graduated
1953

Major accomplishments
Scored 20 points in the championship game of the 1953 state tournament; Received the Trester Award for mental attitude; Indiana All-Star; Indiana University co-captain as a freshman; Indiana Basketball Hall of Famer

Arley, Harley, and Uncle Harold—it's one of the most famous sayings in Indiana high school basketball history. The Andrews boys—Arley and Harley, identical twins, and Harold, a brother of the twins' father—made up three-fifths of the Terre Haute Gerstmeyer starting lineup in the 1952-53 season.

"Yeah, we called Harold, who was nine months younger than Arley and me, Uncle Harold on purpose," said Andrews. "Rather than Uncle taking care of us, we had to take care of Uncle Harold. He played a year after I graduated, and so did Arley because of an accident he had when he was seven and got held back a year."

The Black Cats, who were 30-3 going into the 1953 state tournament finals, lost to South Bend Central, 42-41, in the finals of one of the most controversial championship games ever played at Butler Fieldhouse (now Hinkle Fieldhouse).

Arley wore No. 34, Harley 43, and those numbers, which coach Howard Sharpe often switched to confuse anyone scouting the Black Cats, cost Gerstmeyer dearly. With 5:27 to play, Arley was called for his fifth foul and had to leave the game.

"Most of the season we lucked out by playing five ballplayers 95 percent of the time," said Andrews, who received the Trester Award after the title game, and was inducted into the Indiana Basketball Hall of Fame with Arley in 1989 (Harold, who died three years ago, went into the hall in 1993). "Until tourney time it didn't bother us. But in the finals it did."

Andrews, who led the Black Cats with 20 points, missed a shot with just a few seconds to go, enabling the Bears to hang on for their first state title. However, it was a play in the first half that still haunts the twins.

"It was my brother and I [who were involved in the controversy]," said Andrews. "I made the foul. My brother wasn't within 15 feet of the foul. The official came over and raised my hand. They did that in the state finals that year.

"The only thing is when the official gave the hand signal to the official scorekeeper, he read it in reverse. Rather than 43, he read it as 34, and levied the foul against Arley. That put three on Arley. I maybe had one foul at that time."

Arley got his fourth foul in the first minute of the third quarter. It hurt, said Andrews, because foul No. 5 put the Black Cats in an untenable situation with so much time still to be played. "They took a survey in the press row, and the majority [of the writers] had the foul on me, and not Arley," said Andrews, "but the official scorekeeper would not change [his book]."

Asked if Arley had been able to finish the game, would Gerstmeyer have had a chance to win Terre Haute's first state title, Andrews didn't hesitate to reply in the affirmative.

"We'd have won by 20," he said. "Arley averaged approximately 25 points a game and 11 or so rebounds. He ended up that game with six points and two rebounds." Arley didn't shoot well in the game, but Andrews says, "Eventually his shooting would have caught up to him."

A man with a wry sense of humor, Andrews said, laughing, "While he was out, of course I didn't recognize it, but I had to take over. It did give me a chance to get the ball, and I got to be the leading scorer. South Bend was a good ball club as far as being as tough as the teams we played in the semifinals, and Richmond in the first game of the finals. They were probably not as strong, to be honest, and I'm not downgrading South Bend. We played Evansville Central and Jeffersonville in the semifinals in Bloomington, and they were big ball clubs. We played Richmond in the finals, [and won, 48-40], and they were a big ball club. If South Bend had had to play some of those ball clubs, it would have been tough for them."

Newsmen asked Sharpe about Arley's five-foul count, and he replied, "Gee! Take him out of a state championship with only four fouls!" That was as strong a comment as Sharpe offered to the media. When the subject of Arley's disqualification came up again, Sharpe said, "I don't want to say too much about breaks. I don't want these fellows to think life is cheating them."

Andrews certainly doesn't feel that life cheated him or his teammates by that fateful decision. "That's been our attitude," he said. "It's like in baseball, when a call is made, you accept it. Once that call was made we accepted it."

Gerstmeyer, which is no longer in existence, did not carry a championship trophy back to Terre Haute, and no other Terre Haute school has secured a state title. Did Andrews feel disappointed by the Black Cats' runner-up finish?

"No," he stated. "It's the breaks of the game. It's like the Boston Red Sox. They had their problems before winning the World Series. Terre Haute South went to the state finals three years in a row in the late '70s, and didn't win a title.

"I can't remember which year it was, I think it was 1979, I went to the finals, and Bobby Plump and I sat next to each other since we are Trester Award recipients. That's the year Muncie Central won state with Ray McCallum after beating South in the second afternoon game. I thought South had the best total team, size, speed, and talent of any that came out of Terre Haute. I thought surely that would be the year Terre Haute would bring back a state title, but South got beat."

The Trester Award remains special to Andrews, who says, "After I'm no longer here, then it will be given to the hall of fame by the family. There's no way you can set your mind to win the Trester Award. It's an award given to an athlete. It takes in many facets of an individual's life, his academic background, team effort, his attitude, and character. I was not aware of the award before the game started. And I don't know of many players who are. I learned the true value of the award later. And more as the years go by."

In the December 21, 1953 issue of Life magazine, Harley and Arley were featured in an article. "The first time anybody in high school basketball got a full page in the magazine," said Andrews, the older of the twins by five minutes. He was a freshman at Indiana University, Arley a senior at Gerstmeyer.

"One of my sons had the article bronze plated and put on a walnut board," said Andrews, who is retired from the petroleum business and living in Clay City, Indiana, with his wife Thelma. "It was a nice article."

The twins could have gone to any college they wanted to after leaving Gerstmeyer, says Andrews. He chose Indiana University, while Arley signed with the Philadelphia Phillies as a left-handed pitcher.

"I would have had the opportunity to sign a baseball contract, too, but I wasn't a pitcher," said Andrews. "I played second base and centerfield. I had a good batting average, but there wasn't any money in it unless you were a pitcher. I'd rather take the scholarship [to Indiana University]. Arley played five years and went to the Phillies' training camp every year. During the off-season following his first year, he was in Illinois. Some farmer turned in fornt of Arley and he hit the farmer's vehicle head-on. It ruined his shoulder and pitching career."

Andrews and Hallie Bryant of Indianapolis Attucks High School, were co-captains of the IU freshman team. After a year and a half at IU, Andrews withdrew because he wasn't happy. He went into the military for 33 months, and played a lot of basketball in Austria and Germany while in the special services. He was one of the leading scorers in Europe.

When Andrews returned home, he joined Harold at the University of Louisville. "I was on the basketball team three years, but I didn't play a lot because of a knee injury," he said. "I also played baseball all three years."

Andrews and his wife, Thelma, have two sons, Daryl, 40, and Dennis, 38. Dennis played basketball at South High and Indiana State. Andrews still has business activity in petroleum, but mostly "I do what I want to do. I play golf and work with the Veterans of Foreign Wars. I work at the state level and I've been a district commander."

When asked which of the twins was better, Andrews answered again without hesitation. "Arley," he said. "I think I was a good shooter. There wasn't that much difference in scoring, but he was stronger on the boards than I was. It worked out well, but he was a better all- around athlete. It's been a good life. I've enjoyed all of it."

Arley Andrews

Terre Haute Gerstmeyer High School, Terre Haute

Year graduated
1954

Major accomplishments
Indiana All-Star; Named Terre Haute's best high school basketball
player in a local newspaper survey; Indiana Basketball Hall of Famer

Although fate handed Arley Andrews several cruel setbacks in his early life, the younger of Terre Haute Gerstmeyer's famous twins didn't flinch in the face of adversity and had a most remarkable athletic career.

"I've had some good things happen along the way," said Andrews, who was a year behind his brother Harley in school because of a childhood accident that almost proved fatal. "Basketball, baseball, and my wife Carolyn have been especially good to me."

Carolyn and Andrews have been married 51 years. "She was a cheerleader at Gerstmeyer when I played," he said. "She yelled for me, and now she yells at me; same tone—very firm."

Andrews was named an Indiana All-Star in 1954 along with Bobby Plump, he struck out Mickey Mantle twice in an exhibition baseball game as a flame-throwing left-handed pitcher in the Philadelphia Phillies organization, he led Indiana State in scoring (17.9 average) and rebounding (7.2) in the 1959-60 college basketball season before being declared ineligible for playing professional baseball, and he was chosen in a local newspaper survey Terre Haute's best high school basketball player before consolidation in 1970 eliminated Gerstmeyer, Garfield, Wiley, Schulte, and State high schools. Andrews beat out such talented players as Clyde Lovellette, Terry Dischinger, Bob Leonard, his brother Harley, Charlie Hall, Jim Harness, and Howard Dardeen.

"Bobby Plump and I are friends, and I've played in golf tournaments with him over the years," said Andrews, the only freshman to ever start four years for coach Howard Sharpe at Gerstmeyer—119 games without a miss. "I roomed with Bobby during All-Star week."

Shortly before the 1954 All-Star game in Indianapolis, Andrews signed a Triple A baseball contract with the Phillies. He received a $4,000 signing bonus. Andrews had his career cut short by an auto accident at the end of his first season in the Three-I League. He was driving home to Terre Haute through Illinois when an elderly man driving a large grain truck turned left in front of Andrews' car, causing him to hit the truck head-on, severely injuring his left shoulder. The following season Andrews had surgery on the shoulder at Johns Hopkins University in Baltimore. The pain in Andrews' shoulder became so bad that he "couldn't break a window," and left baseball before completing five seasons. He never even made it to Triple A, but he pitched well in an exhibition game against the Yankees.

"I went five innings and gave up one hit. Yogi Berra got a hit. I struck out Mickey Mantle twice. He'd either strike out or hit a home run against you." Andrews says "without a doubt" he could have made it to the majors if he hadn't gotten hurt. "I had one of the fastest fast balls—95 to 97 mph—in the organization."

When Andrews first played baseball, he attended Indiana State in the off-season. After he left baseball, he joined the Sycamore basketball team. Once again it appeared as though he would have a brilliant college career, but fate brushed back Andrews again.

"I had laid out of basketball almost five years, and it was a little difficult coming back," he said. "But I had a good year with Indiana State [which was in the National Association of Intercollegiate Athletics at the time].

"The following year I was made ineligible. It was because the Olympics were coming up, and anybody that was a pro who had played against some of the other [college] basketball teams could be ineligible. Today you're only pro in the sport you get paid in, and you can play in other sports."

Andrews says he and his brother could have gone almost anywhere in the country to play college basketball. He visited Kansas, Illinois, and was offered a scholarship to West Point. He opted for pro baseball and says that the brevity of his career was a major disappointment.

"I gave up a lot to do it; going to a large university and playing basketball," he said. "It was a tough decision, but I always wanted to play baseball. I would have loved to play a long time. Still, it was a good experience. Off-season, I worked with Tommy John, teaching him how to pitch. He's a Gerstmeyer graduate. I built a mound at my home in north Terre Haute. I built it for myself to rehabilitate a little bit. Tommy's dad would bring him up. We'd work about every evening with him. I taught him quite a bit."

John, a left-hander, too, went on to have an outstanding major league career before he had to have arm surgery that now bears his name. "Several people are having that [Tommy John] surgery and having good luck with it," said Andrews. "I'm sure I could have been taken care of if they had the techniques they have today."

Andrews began to face obstacles early. At age seven, he tripped over a rug on the third floor of the apartment building the family was living in at Chicago and flipped over the railing, suffering a blood clot in the brain when he hit the marble floor. He was laid up long enough that he lost his equilibrium and had to learn to walk all over again.

Perhaps Andrews' most heart-wrenching incident occurred early in the 1953 high school championship game won by South Bend Central, 42-41. He was assessed a foul committed by Harley and fouled out with 5:27 to play, and Gerstmeyer ahead by six points. Andrews was wearing No. 34; Harley had 43. Sharpe had the twins rotate numbers every game.

"I was left-handed, and Harley was right-handed," explained Andrews. "We felt if they scouted us, when we went to play them they would guard us to the right or to the left, and many times that left us an easy way to drive on an individual because they'd be playing the wrong position."

Andrews says there was a mix-up between the referee and official scorekeeper, and he doesn't know to this day whether it was the scorer who put the wrong number down in the book or the referee who signaled the wrong number.

"Sharpe called a timeout immediately and said the foul should have been on Harley," said Andrews. "All the newspapermen on press row agreed, but there wasn't any changing it. And that cost us the ballgame, no doubt about it."

Carolyn remembers well the weeks leading up to the 1953 state tournament finals where Arley, Harley, and their Uncle Harold Andrews would be paired against Richmond, South Bend Central, and Milan at Butler Fieldhouse (now Hinkle Fieldhouse). Gerstmeyer beat Richmond, 48-40, and South Bend Central defeated Milan, 56-37, in the afternoon.

"State-wide all of the newspapers were carrying articles about the famous Andrews twins, and they were referred to as 'Double Trouble,' with pictures of 'em in the newspapers," Carolyn said. "Indianapolis had them in their newspapers all the time. One of the other newspaper pictures had the three boys, Arley, Harley, and Uncle Harold, saying we're ready for a family picnic, getting ready for the finals."

Asked if that meant Gerstmeyer planned to win it all in Indianapolis, Carolyn replied, "Well, that's what the newspaper had captioned the picture as."

Andrews smiled when his wife mentioned the family picnic picture while sitting in their home in east Terre Haute. "No, it wasn't a picnic in the finals," he said.

Do the losses in the 1953 and 1954 state finals still hurt? "It stays with you, not so much the Milan loss, because they beat us by 12 points," said Andrews. "But the South Bend loss was a tough one."

After his college basketball career ended, Andrews went into the oil industry. He lived in Pendleton, but worked out of Anderson 11 years for City Service Oil Co. of Chicago. From there he went with Beam Longest & Neff, an engineering firm in Indianapolis, and was with them 33 years before retiring three years ago. Andrews, who had four bypass heart surgery in July, 2005, and Carolyn have two grown children, Danny and Julie Karn, and two grandchildren.

Harley believes Arley was the better basketball player. "I do think physically I've always been a little heavier and bigger," said Arley. "I think I could do more in rebounding. But I think in shooting we were both the same. I scored a lot more points, but maybe I took more shots. I don't know."

Billy Keller

Washington High School, Indianapolis

Year graduated
1965

Major accomplishments
Named Mr. Basketball; Indiana Basketball Hall of Famer

"Believe it or not, I was born in Bloomington, Indiana," says Billy Keller, who broke his late uncle's heart when he chose to attend Purdue University over Indiana University after leading Indianapolis Washington to the 1965 state high school championship—a victory that helped earn the 5-foot-l0 guard a spot on the Indiana All-Star team as Mr. Basketball.

"Dad worked at Allison's and drove from Bloomington to the west side of Indianapolis. I was about 17 months old when we moved to Indianapolis. Purdue recruited me from my junior year at Washington High. My uncle wanted me to attend IU, but Indiana didn't need additional small guards at that point. It kind of surprises people that I was born in Bloomington and ended up going to Purdue, but it worked out well for me."

Keller, who can be seen driving through Indiana in his red, white, and blue (for the ABA) Billy Keller Basketball Camp van designed by wife Joyce, has been surprising people all of his athletic life. He was advised by his freshman coach at Washington not to go to Purdue because he was too small for the West Lafayette school.

"He wasn't trying to be negative toward Purdue, he was trying to be positive toward me," said Keller. "The more I talked to people, and the more I watched, I felt I could go to Purdue and play, and that I wouldn't get lost."

Keller not only didn't get lost, he helped the Boilermakers win the Big Ten title in 1969 and finish runner-up to UCLA and Lew Alcindor (now Kareem Abdul-Jabbar) in the NCAA tournament. Keller was named the first recipient that year of the James Naismith Award as the nation's most outstanding player under six feet.

A few months later, some of the Indiana Pacers wondered whether Keller would be able to earn a roster spot after being chosen in the eighth round of the 1969 ABA draft. In his seven seasons with the Pacers, Keller earned three championship rings (1970, '72 and '73), averaged 11.8 points for his pro career, and led the team in free-throw percentage, in addition to leading in three-point percentage for four seasons.

Keller, who went into the Indiana Basketball Hall of Fame in 1992, is one of the most popular players ever to wear a Pacers uniform. That popularity became evident in the early 1970s when Norm Wilkens came up with the idea for the song, "The Ballad of Billy Keller." Wilkens had the American Dairy Association account for the Carlson & Co. ad agency. Keller was under contract to the dairy association. Wilkens took his idea to Craig Deitschmann, a producer in Nashville, Tennessee. Deitschmann wrote about 90 percent of the lyrics and the music for the 45 record that was played often on Indianapolis radio station WIBC.

"We sold about 20,000 copies at a dollar apiece," said Wilkens. "That just about covered expenses."

The song had several verses, one of which Wilkens remembers saying, "He stands 5-foot-5 when he starts to drive, but when he takes it in he's like 6-foot-5, that's Bill, Bill Keller, home-grown Hoosier with the red-hot hand."

Wilkens recalls that not only was Keller extremely popular, he also was "kinda shy, but when he made personal appearances at schools around the state for the dairy association, he really turned people on. After he finished, he would stand at mid-court and take a shot at the basket. I don't think in two years he missed more than two shots, and we made 12 to 15 personal appearances each year."

Of his ballad, Keller says, laughing, "I'm sure it wasn't in Casey Kasem's top 40. But I have one at home if anybody would like to hear it. Hey, it's really quite an honor to have your own record."

As Keller's Pacers popularity increased, he was invited to conduct the Indianapolis Symphony Orchestra. "I remember standing on the conductor's stand," he said. "I tapped the stand with my baton to get the musicians' attention, then gave the count and we were off and running." A portion of the ballad was played during a recent Pacers game at Conseco Fieldhouse on a night that honored Keller and some other ABA stars.

Keller also has become a Pacers trivia question. Not long ago, the team's TV announcers, Al Albert and Clark Kellogg, were asking who was second to Reggie Miller in career three-pointers. "It came about that I was second," said Keller with a chuckle. "Al was making light of the fact that Reggie was only about 2,000 ahead of me." Actually the difference is 2,054. Reggie made 2,560, Keller 506. "Reggie had 18 years and I had seven," Keller countered.

Keller's journey to stardom began early. When he was seven, Keller's older brother Bernie would ride Keller's bike to School 67, and make the kid dribble the basketball behind him the mile to the school. Keller was only able to watch the older ones play, but he gained enough knowledge that when he did get to play against his peers, he felt he had an edge.

Vernon McCarty was Keller's coach in junior high school. "He was a very good coach, not only of fundamentals, but of the game itself," said Keller. "He was the guy who gave me my start. Then it was on to Washington and coach Jerry Oliver. He was the same kind of coach—very enthusiastic, and very knowledgeable. And he installed in us to work hard, nothing comes free."

Washington was 29-2 in 1964-65. The Continentals, Princeton, Gary Roosevelt, and Fort Wayne North made up the final four at the state tournament in Butler Fieldhouse (now Hinkle Fieldhouse). Washington, with Keller getting 22 points, defeated Princeton, 88-76, and North beat Roosevelt, 74-65, in afternoon games. Washington downed North, 64-57, as Keller scored 25 points in the championship game.

"When I think about the experience I had at Washington, Ralph Taylor was a big part of that, and so was Eddie Bopp, who was the '65 Trester Award winner," said Keller. "Ralph and I played on the Indiana All-Star team, then went to Purdue together."

Keller says that being named Mr. Basketball was not something he thought much about. "What I thought most about as a kid was two things. I wanted to play on a state championship team, and I wanted to play on the Indiana All-Star team, because at that time there really was only one all-star game. The Indiana-Kentucky All-Star series was, if you will, the grandfather of all all-star games that have ever been played. It wasn't class basketball. It was one class. And because I was shooting for these two dreams—a state title and All-Star game—Mr. Basketball just kind of fell into place."

Keller heard from Indiana, UCLA, Western Kentucky, The Citadel, Butler, Ball State, and Indiana State, but "my heart was with Purdue and [Boilermaker recruiter] Bob King," he said. "I guess to start with, I went for Bob King more than Purdue, because Purdue University to me was Bob King. He was like a father away from home."

Losing to UCLA, 92-72, in the 1969 NCAA championship game was "at the time, probably the most disappointing loss I think I had ever encountered," said Keller. "I think we averaged like 97 points a game with Rick Mount, Herman Gilliam, and George King as our coach. I think had we not had some injuries late in the season, especially with Chuck Bavis not being able to play in the Final Four because of a separated shoulder, and Gilliam just coming back from a leg injury, we would have done much better if we had had all of our parts. I never saw Rick off very often, but he did not shoot well in that final game. He hit his first two, then missed several. You don't know if it's a bad night or you credit the defense. Rick didn't have many bad nights. He really could shoot it."

Some 10 years ago George Faerber, a starting forward on that Purdue team, held a Bee Window grand opening in Lafayette, and with it, a reunion of his teammates. "To that point Herman had never gotten past the fact that we lost to UCLA and they beat us pretty good," said Keller. "I sat down with him and said, yeah, we didn't win, but look what we, and you, accomplished. He'd played eight years in the NBA, had a wonderful career, and won a title with Portland in 1977. Hopefully I was able, while he was alive, [Gilliam died in 2005], to at least get him thinking about the fact that this was a positive experience rather than ending up being a negative one."

Keller was chosen by the Milwaukee Bucks in the NBA draft, and had he made the team he could have played with Abdul-Jabbar, but he thought it would be better to stay at home with the Pacers.

"When you look at that team, you look at the leadership role of coach Bobby Leonard. Slick was very enthusiastic and he loved to have fun, but he loved to win. And he assembled good players. The first one that comes to mind is Roger Brown, then Mel Daniels, Freddie Lewis, Darnell Hillman, Bob Netolicky, and George McGinnis, and guys right on down the line.

Nobody cared who scored the points or got the accolades. I think what people cared about is that we won. I think even today in Indianapolis people still remember the old ABA and the championships we won. That's the foundation of the Indiana Pacers today."

Keller started his camps in 1974 when he played with the Pacers. They were sports camps, but the venture evolved into the Billy Keller Basketball Camp, Inc. He also has a video called "The Lost Art of Shooting," and does individual instruction in addition to conducting mini-shooting schools. He also did some coaching, one year with the Brebeuf Jesuit Preparatory School girls' team, one year as an assistant at Purdue, and seven years with the University of Indianapolis men's team.

Keller and his wife, Joyce, have two grown daughters, four grand-children, and "three granddogs." And the man who inspired a ballad doesn't think being 5-10 held him back in any way.

"I don't feel like the players today are any better at their game than we were at our game," he said. "Sometimes people want to say our [Pacers] team back in the '70s, how could you compete? Well, you can't compare that. But I feel we were as good, and at this point we accomplished more in our game then than the teams today have accomplished."

Ralph Taylor

Washington High School, Indianapolis

Year graduated
1965

Major accomplishments
**Ranked third in career rebounds (1,020) for Washington;
Named an Indiana All-Star; Secretary of the Indiana Hall of Fame;
Indiana Basketball Hall of Famer**

Ralph Taylor's journey to the Indiana Basketball Hall of Fame had a most unusual beginning.

"My first love was baseball," said the 2001 inductee who helped Indianapolis Washington High School win the 1965 state championship, and Purdue finish runner-up to UCLA in the 1969 NCAA tournament. "I was a big Dodgers fan. I wanted to be like Duke Snider, or Sandy Koufax, or Jackie Robinson. I played baseball and softball in Military Park, then gradually I got into basketball."

Taylor was not a can't-miss basketball prospect as a sixth grader on the School 5 team. "I had trouble figuring out which was the right basket to shoot at," he said. "I think I scored four points in two different games for the other team."

In the seventh grade, Taylor learned to shoot at the right basket, and has remained on target ever since in becoming an Indiana All-Star, a member of the Hall of Fame's Silver Anniversary team in 1990, and one of the four all-time favorite players in Purdue basketball history. Taylor, program director of the Central Indiana Community Foundation in

Indianapolis for the past six years, didn't become aware that he was a Purdue favorite until about a decade ago when a book detailing the history of Boilermaker basketball came out.

"I owe a lot of my early success in basketball to Clifford Robinson, who replaced Jumpin' Johnny Wilson—Mr. Basketball from Anderson in 1946, as the School 5 coach after my fifth grade year," said Taylor, who became secretary of the Hall of Fame in July, 2005 (he stands to become the first African American president of the Hall in 2009). "He left to become the third African American to become head coach at an Indiana high school—Indianapolis Wood."

By the time he was a seventh grader, says Taylor, Robinson had him to the point "where I could figure out the right basket to shoot at."

Taylor not only was a Dodger fan, he was a Crispus Attucks fan and "just knew I was going there." It didn't happen. He didn't realize that his house south of New York Street was just outside of the Attucks boundary. Taylor later found out he would be sent to Washington by someone in charge of student personnel placement in the Indianapolis Public School system.

"Going to Washington turned out to be a good thing," said Taylor. "I remember the first time playing against Attucks my freshman year at Washington it was like stabbing your brother in the back. It was always the team I had dreamed of playing for. They never beat us in my four years at Washington."

Although he played center for the Continentals at 6-foot-2, Taylor was a rebounding dynamo. He ranks third in career rebounds (1,020) at Washington behind George McGinnis and Steve Downing.

"In four years at Washington, I was on teams that were never out-rebounded," he said. "I was never out-rebounded by any other center—that I know for a fact. I always knew my height was actually to my advantage, because if someone was taller they'd look at me, and say there's no way he can out-rebound me. Also, it was a matter of God-given ability to jump, as well as being fundamentally sound on blocking out."

Washington's success in 1965 came as a bit of a surprise to Taylor, because he feels the '64 team was the best of the two. But in the afternoon game of the '64 sectional, he injured his knee against Wood and didn't play in the title game against Howe.

"We had beaten Howe by about 13 points earlier in the season," he said. "We had a couple of other players that were dealing with injuries, so we were not at full strength, and lost."

Taylor and Billy Keller were the only returning lettermen on the '65 team. "But everything came together," said Taylor. "We had great chemistry and great leadership with Jerry Oliver [head coach], Dick Harmening [assistant coach], and Howard Leedy, who was like a volunteer assistant coach. The two teams that beat us during the season—Manual and Ben Davis—we wound up beating in the tournament."

Taylor remembers sitting in the Continentals' dressing room in Butler Fieldhouse waiting to play Ben Davis in the semistate, and overhearing comments from Ben Davis players in a nearby dressing room. "I think they thought they were going to beat us again," said Taylor. "We sat there very quietly waiting for the game to start. And we knew we'd kick their butt when it did."

In the state finals, Washington defeated Princeton, 88-76, in the first afternoon game and Fort Wayne North upset Gary Roosevelt, 74-65, in the second contest. The Continentals beat North, 64-57, in the title game to earn Washington its first state championship, and to finish the season with a 29-2 record.

"The thing that stuck out to me in the state finals was I didn't realize I was attracting so much defensive attention," said Taylor, who carried a 17-point average into the finals. "The good thing about that was despite the double and triple teaming on me, I think it allowed the other players to really help us win the state championship. We had wanted to play Gary Roosevelt, but met North instead. Both teams were really tight. It was a dismal performance the first half. We played our press the whole second half and that caused us to win."

North played a zone defense, and every time Taylor got the ball he says he was "surrounded by a forest. I couldn't hit anything and had a bad performance. But Billy Keller, Marv Winkler, and Eddie Bopp came through as they always did." Taylor had 15 points against Princeton, and 13 versus North.

Taylor calls the love for the Washington team unreal. "The support we had, not only from the Washington fans, the students, adult alumni, and the entire city of Indianapolis was tremendous. I've run into people who didn't even live in Indianapolis, and they'd say it was just a joy to watch our team perform."

Taylor received several college offers, but says his guidance counselor didn't give him all the letters. "I think she kinda wanted Billy and I to stay close to Indianapolis. We both wound up going to Purdue. Bob King, who did most of Purdue's recruiting, sold us on the Boilermakers. It's hard to say no to somebody like that."

As a Purdue freshman, Taylor was the team's leading rebounder and second-leading scorer. He never started on the varsity, playing little as a sophomore, but more as a junior and senior.

"My Purdue career wasn't what I expected from a playing standpoint. But in terms of maturation, friendships, and getting a college degree [in education], I think it was great. My senior year was our best team. The chemistry was outstanding. It was similar to the Washington experience. Once the momentum picked up we became like the darlings of West Lafayette and Lafayette."

In the 1969 Final Four at Louisville, Kentucky, UCLA narrowly beat Drake, 85-82, and Purdue breezed by North Carolina, 92-65. The championship game was a far different story. UCLA defeated Purdue by 20 points, 92-72.

"Chuck Bavis hurt his shoulder against Miami of Ohio," said Taylor. "He had had good success against Lew Alcindor, who later became Kareem Abdul-Jabbar. So our two [remaining] centers were 6'9" and combined, barely weighed 400 pounds. Chuck weighed about 260, so he was able to use his weight against Alcindor.

"We thought we had a fairly good chance to beat UCLA. But that was the day Rick [Mount] probably had the worst game of his career, and Herm Gilliam was dealing with an injury. It wasn't meant to be."

Taylor remembers returning to the Purdue campus after the game, and upon seeing all of the fans who greeted them, feeling good about his four years as a Boilermaker. "We'd come home from road trips early in the season, and the only people there would be our girlfriends or somebody wondering why we were at the airport. That changed after we came back from a road trip when we beat Iowa, and we see all these people, and we tried to figure out why they were there. They were there for us, and it was like we had finally arrived—where basketball was now kinda on the same level as football."

After graduation, Taylor taught for three years in IPS (two at Washington), spent 17 years with the Purdue Extension Service in Marion County, worked four years as recreation administrator for the Indianapolis Parks Department, and five years for the Indiana Youth Institute before going to the CICF.

"I feel blessed," said Taylor, "because I was born in what I would call the golden era of Indiana high school basketball, and the birth of the popularity of basketball at Purdue. Now, I've reaped the benefits of all that."

Brad Miley

Rushville High School, Rushville

Year graduated
1976

Major accomplishments
Holds a two-game final four record of 45 rebounds, and a one-game
record of 29 rebounds; Indiana All-Star

Brad Miley was not a happy camper when his father moved the family
from Speedway to Rushville to take a job in an air conditioning
business in the summer of 1975.

"I'll be the first to say that when it happened I was like any 17-year-old
kid, I wanted to stay at Speedway, having grown up there," said Miley, who's
been in the wholesale beverage business with the Olinger Distributing Co. for
a little over 20 years, and coaching his two sons in AAU basketball in his free
time.

"I wanted to stay with my friends, and with my coach there, Morris
Pollard. My dad, of course, which I probably would do the same with my kids,
made me go with him. Looking back, it was the best thing that ever happened
to me."

The move not only helped Miley become an Indiana All-Star in 1976, it
was instrumental in getting him to his present residence, Terre Haute, where
he was a starting forward, and a teammate of Larry Bird during Indiana State's
near-perfect college season of 1978-79. Even though Miley wanted to remain
a Speedway Sparkplug rather than become a Rushville Lion in his high school
senior season, he soon realized he was walking into a promising situation.

"What was ironic was that Rushville had four kids coming back after losing to Columbus North in the final game of the Indianapolis semistate in 1975," he said. "I was a perfect fit, being 6-foot-8, to fill the middle."

Miley played with the Goins brothers for coach Larry Angle. Rick Goins also made the Indiana All-Star team in '76, and his brother Dennis, who started at point guard as a freshman in the '75-'76 season, made the All-Star team in 1979.

"Rick Goins and I made a nice inside-outside tandem," said Miley. "He was about 6-foot-5 as a guard. We had two 6-foot-4 forwards, so we were a fairly big team." And talented—the Lions were 25-1 going into the state tournament finals at Market Square Arena in Indianapolis.

Rushville drew East Chicago Washington in its afternoon game. The Senators went into the finals ranked No. 1, and with a 25-game winning streak. The Lions appeared overmatched early, falling behind, 33-12, at the end of the first quarter, but Miley and mates rallied to win, 68-59, in one of the most memorable games in tournament history. The late IHSAA commissioner, Phil Eskew, exclaimed afterward, "Did you ever in your life see anything like it?" Then he added, "And that rebounding by Miley! Why, that must be a record."

Miley had a personal best of 29 rebounds, which remains a one-game record for the state tournament finals. "East Chicago never slowed down the game when they had the lead," he said. "There were rebounds to be had. I also had 17 points, five blocked shots, two steals, and one assist. So I had a very active game."

In the championship game, which Marion won, 82-76, for a second consecutive title, Miley remembered having 21 rebounds, which would have given him 50 for a two-game record, and 19 points. According to IHSAA records, Miley only had 16 rebounds, giving him 45, which still gave him a two-game record.

The IHSAA takes responsibility for the discrepancy. The 21-rebound total Miley mentioned having in the championship game appeared in the program for the 2005 state tournament. "We went back to the box scores in the 1975-76 yearbook and found it was 16 rebounds, which gave Miley 45 for the day, a two-game record," said Joe Gentry, IHSAA public relations director.

Miley is understandably proud of breaking the state finals rebound records set by George McGinnis of Indianapolis Washington High in 1969 (27 for one game, 43 for two games), but he is humble about the accomplishment.

"My parents moved to Holland, Michigan, from Rushville, and lived there for years until my dad passed away," he said. "Mom now lives in Terre

Haute, but when she lived in Holland she would call me every March. About the only thing she was concerned about was whether the single-game record still stood. She would say, 'Did it get broken? Did it get broken?'"

Those records, plus Rushville's outstanding 1975-76 season, didn't escape the recruiters. Miley made visitations to Indiana State, Arkansas and Auburn. His parents wanted him to stay in state so they could watch him play, and he remembers how his visit to ISU convinced him that Birdland was the right choice for him.

"Having met Larry the first time down at campus and playing with him the week I visited I knew right then that's where I wanted to be," said Miley. "He was something like you'd never seen before. He was the ultimate team player. You always hear about some players making other players better. He did."

ISU went 25-3, 23-9, 33-1, and 16-11 in Miley's four years. As a freshman, he was sixth man until the final game of the season, an 83-82 loss to Houston and Otis Birdsong in the NIT.

"I'll never forget, [coach] Bob King said to me, 'If you can hold Otis under 30, we win the game.' He got 30 on the button, and we lost by one. It was a real experience for me at the time being an 18-year-old kid playing against a senior in college. Then I started my sophomore, junior, and senior years."

Miley's forte was defense and rebounding. "That was a perfect fit for our team, and that's what I did four years. I was playing against the best player in the world at the time is the way I looked at it. I was seeing things in a game, like nothing compared to what I see every day. I said to myself, 'If I can hold my own against [Bird], there's a lot of people I can affect.'"

One of Miley's most significant rebounds came with three seconds left in a game at New Mexico State on February 1, 1979. He took one dribble and passed to Bob Heaton at mid-court. Heaton banked in a 52-foot shot that tied the game, and ISU won in overtime to extend its unbeaten streak to 19-0. The shot earned Heaton the nickname Miracle Man.

"Larry fouled out on the play that gave a New Mexico State player a one-and-one free throw situation," said Miley. "What was amazing at the time is that I got the rebound, and Bob was wide open. I think that they were thinking the kid who was shooting was an 80-percent foul shooter, and he was gonna make 'em. They relaxed, so Bob was able to get off a pretty good release with nobody in his face."

In the Sycamores' five games in the 1979 NCAA tournament, the last of which ISU lost to Michigan State and Magic Johnson, 75-64, to finish 33-1,

Miley was 9-of-10 from the field, 0-of-4 from the foul line, scored 18 points and had 20 rebounds. Not great statistics, but still very significant.

"Whether people want to give me credit for it, I think I'm the leading field-goal percentage shooter in Indiana State history [for a season in 1978-79, .630 on 74-of-118]," said Miley. "Of course, I never got outside five or six feet of the basket. It was a bonus playing with a guy like Larry, because when he made his moves he would make the right delivery to you. All you had to do was catch it and you probably had a lay-up. So many kids playing the game now don't understand that one person who makes that sacrifice can be the difference in the game for you."

After college, Miley played professionally overseas for five seasons; two in Australia and three in Iceland. "I went from the bottom of the world to the top, and had a ball at both locations," he said. When Miley returned to the U.S., he played with Bill Cook's traveling team of Bloomington until he was 36.

Miley was a runner-up in two of Indiana's most famous basketball games, in high school and college. He thinks about it a lot, but says, "I wouldn't trade my high school and college days for the world."

Eric Montross

Lawrence North High School, Indianapolis

Year graduated
1990

Major accomplishments
Scored 40 points in final four of the 1989 state tournament and had 18 rebounds in the 1989 state tournament title game; Named Indiana All-Star in 1990; Set 10 individual scoring records as a Wildcat

After setting 10 individual records in scoring, rebounding, and blocked shots at Lawrence North High School of Indianapolis in addition to leading the Wildcats to the 1989 state championship, Eric Montross took a walk down Tobacco Road following his senior year in 1990 when he was an Indiana All-Star.

Not only did the 7-footer find happiness and success at Chapel Hill, North Carolina—as a junior he helped the North Carolina Tar Heels win the NCAA championship in 1993—Montross found a second home. He currently resides in Chapel Hill with his wife, Laura, a native of Lexington, North Carolina, and their two children, Andrew, seven, and Sarah, five. In addition to professional speaking and conducting leadership seminars, Montross keeps busy doing radio commentary for Tar Heel games.

What has life on Tobacco Road meant to Montross, who spent 10 active years in the NBA for six different teams; including the Boston Celtics who drafted Montross as the ninth pick in the 1994 draft?

"It was a perfect follow up to growing up in the hotbed of Hoosier high school basketball; which I guess you could compare to Texas football, prior to the class split, which I think is a travesty. For me, it was going from the best high school arena for basketball into the best arena for college basketball, which is the Duke/North Carolina State/Wake Forest rivalry with North Carolina."

Montross says being coached by Dean Smith at North Carolina was an added bonus, "because he gave everything he had to his team, and loved his team, and we loved him. I feel like I was taught a great deal about the game of basketball from my father, and from Jack Keefer and Dave Erwin at Lawrence North; but when I was exposed to the next level of coaching and dedication to the sport—and that was headed by coach Smith—I feel like I became a more polished player, and had more of a clear and concise understanding of just what it meant to play the game of basketball, not just to put the ball in the hoop."

As Montross looks back on his Tobacco Road experience, he calls it "very storybook. And I'll even include being drafted by the Celtics as kind of icing on the cake. You go from Indiana high school basketball to North Carolina and Dean Smith for college basketball, to the tradition of the Boston Celtics and being on the team that once was coached by Red Auerbach."

That's an incredible journey for someone who was recruited "by every Division I school." Montross says that his dealings with Bob Knight, then coach at Indiana University, were positive. "I had a great deal of respect for his coaching ability. That was never a question. A lot of people gave me guff, some even said I was a traitor for going out of state. The fact is, it's a very selfish decision to go to college. For me there was no question that North Carolina was where I was going to be most comfortable academically and athletically."

As a Tar Heel, Montross played twice in Indianapolis: while a freshman at the RCA Dome in the NCAA Final Four in 1991; and as a junior at Hinkle Fieldhouse, where the Tar Heels defeated Butler, 103-56. Montross remembers little about his first Final Four experience.

"In a large part, I was more excited about being back at home with family and friends than I was about being in the Final Four, because I had come off a very successful high school career," he said. "I came to Carolina and went to the Final Four, and I thought, 'Man, this is just how it is.' I had no idea of the magnitude of what that team had achieved, even though we were knocked out by Kansas in the first game. That was one of those things that you look back on and you think, 'Gosh, kid, wake up and smell the coffee.'"

Montross certainly smelled the coffee in the 1992-93 season. Of his trip to Hinkle Fieldhouse, where Montross played in the sectional, regional, and semistate as a Wildcat, he says, "It had the smell of a gym, and playing there during the day, with the sun coming through the windows at the top of the bleachers, was special. It was the most amazing atmosphere I ever played in."

The 1993 Final Four in New Orleans' Super Dome earned Montross a second championship ring to go with the one that he had earned as a Wildcat. He scored 23 points in UNC's opening victory over Kansas. The final game against Michigan became famous because Chris Webber called for a time out late when the Wolverines had no time outs remaining. Donald Williams, named the game's MVP, sank two free throws to clinch the Tar Heel victory.

"I believe our team was strong enough to win, even without Webber's help," said Montross. "Folks reading it may not believe it, but I think, from our perspective, we were such a disciplined ball club; we were used to close games. We had confidence in each other, we had confidence in coach Smith, coach [Bill] Guthridge and the rest of the assistants."

After the victory, Montross joined other teammates in videotaping the celebration that night and the next day at Chapel Hill. "I've probably replayed it four or five times," he said. "Every time I play it, I look a little goofier and the tape gets a little more meaningful."

Montross gives Lawrence North Coach Keefer and his former assistant, Erwin, full credit for helping him prepare for those savory moments during and after the Final Four. Keefer had a saying that good guards win games, good centers win games, but good guards and good centers win championships. Guard Todd Leary scored 26 points, and center Montross had 19 points and 18 rebounds in Lawrence North's 74-57 victory over Kokomo in the '89 state championship game.

"Coach Keefer gave me challenges that I taped to my wall in my room growing up," said Montross. "And every day that we didn't have a game, Erwin worked with me in the morning from 6:30 to 7:30 a.m. After we finished, I'd run in, take a shower, change, then race to my first-period class still sweating. It was the repetition and his dedication to meet me every morning that I really appreciated."

In February 2004, Montross had reconstructive surgery on his left ankle after feeling what he thought was a little foot cramp while going up the stairs before a game against Detroit. It turned out to be more serious than a cramp—bone chips had caused a bone bruise or stress fracture. Montross opted for reconstructive surgery rather than undergoing a more significant surgery that may or may not have gotten to the bone chips. Although the surgery has helped, Montross hasn't been able to play again.

"I'm disappointed that I can't play again," he said. "The good thing is I feel like I'm pretty balanced in that the other huge part of my life—besides basketball—my family. I think the silver lining here is that whatever stopped me was one of those things that maybe saved my ability to walk without a limp for the rest of my life.

"It's very satisfying to look at the opportunities I had to play with some of the best players, to be coached by some of the best coaches, and to live every kid's dream of playing in the NBA for 10 years. That's something I feel very fortunate about. I certainly have some remorse that I couldn't play longer, but have no negative feelings about my career."

Does Montross consider himself a Tar Heel or a Hoosier? He laughed and said, "There's an old saying, 'A Tar Heel born, a Tar Heel bred, and when I die, I'm a Tar Heel dead.' I'll probably go down as being a Hoosier born, a Hoosier bred, and when I die, I'll be a Tar Heel dead. But I will always consider Indianapolis home. Chapel Hill is my mid-life stop."

Larry Humes

Madison High School, Madison

Year graduated
1962

Major accomplishments
Mr. Basketball; All-American three years; Indiana Basketball Hall of Famer

After the spotlights came on for the introduction of the Madison High School Cubs in the late '50s and early '60s, coach Bud Ritter's teams played nearly perfect basketball.

"We were ahead of our time," said Larry Humes, star of the 1959, '60, '61 and '62 Madison teams that went 97-5 with only one regular-season loss. "One of the polka-dot uniforms that we wore is in a case at Conseco Fieldhouse in Indianapolis. It's mine. I wore 44 in high school. They didn't have a 44, so they put a 14 in there. And now all NBA teams use spotlights to introduce their teams."

Ritter's teams were not only ahead of time basketball-wise, they were ahead of time socially. A white coach who moved to Madison from Peru fully integrated the team when Humes arrived at high school as a freshman.

"I was very fortunate," said Humes, who became Mr. Basketball after the Cubs lost their only game of the 1961-62 season to the eventual state champion, Evansville Bosse, 79-75. "Bud Ritter came to town three or four years before I got to high school. He saw talent in me, and worked with me specially. I'm grateful he did, because he's the reason I played basketball."

As a youth Humes played only in his backyard and the parks. "Blacks got the gym one hour a week on Tuesday night," he said. "I did some history, and there was one black that practiced with the team when Madison won the state championship in 1950, but they never dressed him. He never got a ring, and they said he was just as good as the guys on there. A few years later they had a guy they dressed but he played very little. He had a younger brother who played some."

Ritter, says Humes, didn't see color in his players, only talent. "Bud Ritter had open eyes, and he was going to play the best players and have the best teams possible. I was the first black to play all the time. I started all four years and I owe that to Bud Ritter. Basketball was very, very good to me. That was a way I could have better things and learn about the world and people in general, and turn negative things into positive things."

Five of Humes' seven brothers played basketball after him at Madison. Howard, known as "Bugsy," was an Indiana All-Star in 1965, and went to Indiana State. Willie Humes went to Idaho State.

In Humes' freshman season, the Cubs went to the semistate in Butler Fieldhouse. "That was really something," he said, "because I was scared to death. Coming from a small town like Madison, Butler Fieldhouse was one of the biggest places I'd ever seen. I had 19 points against Crispus Attucks. We lost, 82-80, in overtime."

A year later Madison advanced again to the semistate in Butler Fieldhouse. The Cubs defeated Rushville, 74-60, but lost to Muncie Central and Ron Bonham, 73-64, in the championship game.

As a senior in 1962, Humes finally got a semistate victory. The Cubs defeated Connersville, 73-64, and Anderson, 91-81. That sent undefeated Madison to the state finals in Butler Fieldhouse. East Chicago Washington, Kokomo, and Evansville Bosse were the other finalists.

"We beat Bosse during the regular season, 59-51, then they came back in the tournament and upset us, 79-75," said Humes. "Bosse was on our regular schedule all the time, because Bud Ritter was from Evansville and went to Bosse. Evansville Bosse was the fourth team picked to win the title. It was a very big disappointment that we lost, because all young kids want to win the state title. We just didn't play quite up to our capabilities. I was one game away from getting a silver or gold ring, and never got it. But after that disappointment, I got Mr. Basketball, which helped it a little bit. As a team you want to win the state finals, and as an individual, Mr. Basketball is the highest honor you can get."

Humes was captain of the Indiana All-Star team that split with Kentucky. He was named Star of Stars.

"I had many choices of college," said Humes. He narrowed his list to Purdue, because Ray Eddy was the coach and he was from Madison and had coached the Cubs; Cincinnati; UCLA; and Evansville College (now the University of Evansville).

"I went to Evansville," Humes added. "I was young and I really didn't know. Bud Ritter thought Evansville would be the best place for me. He was from there, and basketball was great there. The school had great education, and Arad McCutchan was a great coach. Bud Ritter knew Mr. McCutchan, so I took Ritter's word for it and went to Evansville. I haven't regretted it since. It's probably the best move I've ever made. The other schools were bigger, but what I accomplished, the people I came in contact with, and the things I learned just in life itself—it probably was the best place for me."

Humes didn't disappoint his high school coach. He wasn't eligible for the varsity as a freshman, but he won NCAA Division II championships as a sophomore and junior. The Purple Aces defeated Akron, 72-59, in the championship game of 1964, and beat Southern Illinois, 85-82, in overtime in the '65 title game. Humes was an All-American three years, and he holds just about all of the school's offensive records. That includes season points (941); career field goals (865); season free throws (227); career scoring average (26.4); and season scoring average (32.5).

The Purple Aces were 26-3 in 1964, and 29-0 in '65. "Those two years I really think we were one of the top teams in the country, Division I or II," said Humes. "We played a lot of Division I schools in the preseason: New Mexico State, Arizona, Iowa, Purdue, Columbia, Northwestern, Notre Dame, George Washington, Louisiana State, and Massachusetts.

"Our preseason was a lot tougher than our conference season. Jerry Sloan was a very good defensive player, and I was the offensive player. We really meshed." Sloan had an outstanding career with the Chicago Bulls, and is the longtime coach of the Utah Jazz in the NBA.

A few years ago, the top 15 players in Evansville history were named, and Humes was ranked No. 1. His jersey has been retired and hangs from the rafters in Roberts Stadium, along with the jerseys of Gus Doerner, Sloan, and Don Buse. Humes is also in the Evansville and Indiana Halls of Fame.

If the Madison uniforms were different, so were the Purple Aces'. During Humes' tenure in Evansville he wore No. 50 emblazoned on a T-shirt, and when he went to the bench, he put on a robe, not a sweat shirt.

"Back then the gyms were very cold, not like they are now," he said. "So the robes were very, very nice, because once you came out you were very warm, and the robes helped you stay warm. I didn't like the T-shirts at first, but once I got there I liked them, because they kept you very warm. And they didn't bother your shooting. About five years ago, they went to the regular jersey, and I'm sorry they did. They should have kept that tradition."

After being drafted by Chicago in 1966, Humes survived until the final cut before the season began. He would have made $10,000 if he had made the team, but he did receive a $2,000 bonus. "I thought that was a lot of money, and back then it was decent," said Humes. "It was very disappointing, not making the team, but it probably was the best thing that ever happened to me."

Soon after his basketball days ended, Humes embarked on a teaching and coaching career in Indianapolis that spanned 40 years. He retired in 2005. Humes taught one year in a middle school, then spent five years each at Shortridge High School and Howe High School as a basketball assistant.

Humes' next move was to his alma mater as a basketball assistant. He worked at scouting and recruiting through the summer of 1977, then fate smiled on him. The Crispus Attucks high school job opened up and he took it. "I had never been a head coach, and I said, 'Well, I'm going to see how I do as my own boss.'" Not long after he accepted the job, a plane carrying the Purple Aces team and coaches to a game crashed, killing all onboard.

Humes coached at Attucks for 10 years. Then the school was made a middle school. He went from Attucks to the University of Indianapolis, and spent six years there as an assistant. When Bill Green was let go as the Greyhounds coach, Royce Waltman was hired. Humes said, "I'd been there long enough, so I went back to IPS (Indianapolis Public Schools)."

Humes and his wife, Cecele, have a son, Larry Jr., and a daughter, Shannon. Larry Jr. works for the Marion County Health Department and Shannon manages a pharmacy in Dallas. Cecele is secretary at an Indianapolis middle school.

Evansville didn't give rings when Humes helped the school win consecutive NCAA titles in the '60s. "They gave us watches," he said. "I still have one watch. I had one watch made into a necklace for my wife. I do have my Mr. Basketball ring," and a lot of wonderful memories.

Don Buse

Holland High School, Holland

Year graduated
1968

Major accomplishments
Indiana All-Star; Indiana Basketball Hall of Famer

The numbers game was never a deterrent in Don Buse's outstanding basketball career. Although there were only 21 students in the Huntingburg native's Holland High School graduation class in 1968, he averaged 22 points and 14 rebounds for the Dutchmen in his senior season when they were unbeaten through the sectional.

Holland met Oolitic, which also was unbeaten, in the afternoon game of the regional and won. In the championship game, the Dutchmen lost to Jeffersonville by two points. Fortunately, Buse's credentials were good enough to warrant selection to the Indiana All-Star team. Indiana lost twice to Kentucky that year, but Buse's experience in the All-Star series was a disappointment.

"I didn't get much playing time," he said. "I don't know what the deal was. I guess Cleon Reynolds, [the Indiana coach], didn't think I could play. I think that I only got a couple of minutes in each game. It was strange when I look back at it."

While pursuing a college site, the 6-foot-4 Buse visited Jacksonville, Alabama, Western Kentucky, and Kentucky Wesleyan. "I had a chance to visit Oklahoma," said the man nicknamed "Boo." "John McLeod [a Hoosier] was coach there. He eventually coached the Phoenix Suns, where I played for a while. But I had visited so many schools, so I called him and said, 'John, I'm getting more confused as I go.' I didn't want to go that far away from home. Evansville had a good basketball reputation and program, and that's one of the reasons I went there."

As an Ace, Buse was Indiana Collegiate Conference player of the year twice (1971 and '72), and All-American in 1972. In 1971, Evansville won the NCAA Division II national championship, beating Old Dominion, 97-82, in the title game.

"I've got a ring," said Buse. "I think it looks identical to the rings the Division I guys get. It was quite a thrill."

Buse played for Arad McCutchan at Evansville, who coached the Aces for 31 years. What was it like playing for the man who won six NCAA Division II national championships?

"He was kind of a basketball legend," said Buse. "When I played there, he was getting up in age a little bit. He was pretty much set in his ways. He didn't like to play any zone. But he was successful as a coach. You have to give him credit for that. And when you came out of a game, they'd put that robe on you. Arad thought you could get that off real quick if you went into the game. And I think he thought they kept you warmer. They did."

Late in his freshman season, Buse began to room with Steve Welmer, also a freshman from Columbus who has become one of the nation's premier officials. "We kinda hit it off and got along real good," said Buse. "If you know Steve Welmer, you've gotta like him. He's a character, and I think an excellent official."

Buse was selected in the third round of both the NBA and ABC drafts of 1972. He was chosen by Phoenix of the NBA, and the Virginia Squires of the ABA. Before the start of the 1972-73 season, the Pacers acquired Buse's rights. He did not have a no-cut contract, but made the team.

"I was pleased when I heard I was going to Indiana," said Buse, "because it gave me a chance to play close to home. I didn't know a whole lot about the Pacers, but I knew they had a very good team. I was lucky enough to win a title my first year."

Buse says he had a good relationship with coach Bob Leonard, a relationship that continues to this day. "Slick and I are still good friends," he said. "I enjoyed playing for him. I thought he was a good coach. He comes down to Huntingburg about every summer, and spends four or five days. We take in the horses races and talk old times."

Buse has named a three-year-old horse he bred on his farm in southern Indiana Big Daddy Slick after Leonard, who is nicknamed Slick. He owns the horse with Charlie Hobgood, a friend from his days at the University of Evansville. Big Daddy Slick will probably make his debut in the fall of 2006 at Hoosier Park in Anderson.

Buse played 13 seasons as a professional, four in the ABA with the Pacers, and nine in the NBA—three with the Pacers, three with Phoenix, one with Portland, and his final two seasons with Kansas City.

"I had a lot of fun playing basketball," said Buse. "I don't know of any job I'd rather had than playing basketball, because really it wasn't like a job. It was just something you loved to do.

"I didn't score a lot. I was probably known more as a defensive player and a playmaker—a guy passing the ball. I probably did turn down a lot of shots in my career. If you go back, I think everybody would do something different. But that's water under the bridge. I probably would have tried to score more."

Buse averaged 7.1 points, 4.6 assists and 1.9 steals in 966 regular-season games. He led the ABA in minutes played in 1975-76 with Indiana—3,380 for an average of 40.2, also a league high in the last ABA season. In addition, Buse led the league that season in assists with 689, and steals with 346. In the next season, Indiana's first in the NBA, Buse led the league in assists with 685, and steals with 281.

Buse's defensive prowess began to show prominently in the 1976-77 season with Indiana, when he was named a first team all-defensive player. He repeated that feat the next three seasons with Phoenix. Buse credits his high school coach with making him sound fundamentally, and willing to expend the necessary energy to make him strong defensively.

"You have to be willing to work hard on defense, and I did," said Buse. "A lot of that was taught to me by my high school coach, Woody Neal. I give him a lot of credit for my success. He worked you extremely hard. He also was a disciplinarian. I don't think any team that we played was in any better physical condition than we were. He really ran you in practice, and I think that gave us an advantage. We were a small school. If we had to go seven players we were a little bit thin. We had to be in shape, and most of the starters basically played the whole game."

The Pacers traded Buse to Phoenix after the 1976-77 season, and he spent three enjoyable years with the Suns. "I really liked Phoenix," he said.

"John McLeod, who tried to get me to go to Oklahoma when I was at Holland, was coaching Phoenix at the time, and we had a very good team. In the 1978-79 season, we finished two games behind Seattle in the Pacific Division. We lost to Seattle in the seventh game of the conference finals. Seattle went on to win the NBA title. That was a disappointing thing when I look back. I felt we had the talent, and should have won the whole ball of wax."

After the 1979-80 season, Buse was traded back to Indiana. Following the next season, he ran into a contract problem with the Pacers. "They didn't renew my contract," he said. "They wanted me to take a big pay cut. I wasn't making that much to start with. So I sat out half of that season. Portland had a guard get hurt about mid-way through the season, and I signed with them. After that I finished my last two years in Kansa City. I didn't know much about Kansas City, and they didn't draw real well. They weren't as successful as the other teams I had played for, but like I said, I enjoyed every place I went."

During his second season in Kansas City, his 13th overall, Buse started to get a few more injuries than normal. "I separated my shoulder, and I had a pulled hamstring," he said. "I probably could have played another year or two, but I thought, well, maybe it's time to hang it up."

Buse moved back to Evansville and bought a condo. In the meantime, he received a telephone call from Cotton Fitzsimmons, his coach at Kansas City, who wanted Buse to assist him in San Antonio. He did for one season, then helped Jerry Reynolds with the Sacramento Kings after Fitzsimmons got fired.

"Then I went back to southern Indiana," said Buse, whose roots are deep there. In 1989 he built a log house on 25 acres five miles outside Huntingburg and four miles outside Holland. He's divorced and lives by himself. Buse has a 21-year-old son.

Buse is in his third stint as an assistant basketball coach at Southridge High School, a consolidation of Holland and Huntingburg, and he is in the horse business.

"I've owned thoroughbreds for quite a long time," he said. "It's enjoyable. You've gotta get up and go feed them. I clean the stalls. It's something you do every day. The coaching and the horses, that's about all I'm doing.

"I've won a few races. I'd love to get in the Kentucky Derby, but that's hard to do. I don't have the resources to go over and buy one of those yearling sales horses. I'm mainly into Indiana-bred horses. I'm concerned about racing in Indiana, at Shelbyville and at Anderson."

Buse says he made a good living in pro basketball, but adds, "It was nothing like it is today. I hope these guys today realize how good they've got it. It's amazing the kind of money they're making. My signing bonus with the Pacers was $3,000. I remember that because I owed that on a Volkswagen that I bought in my senior year in college. That paid off my car."

Don's contract as a Pacer rookie was for around $23,000. "I don't know what the minimum salary is right now in the NBA, but I bet it is more than I made in my highest year ever. They have a different life style in the NBA than when I was playing."

Even so, Buse says, "It's been a good life. I wouldn't trade it for anything."

Mike Weaver

Huntington High School, Huntington

Year graduated
1964

Major accomplishments
Received the Trester Award for mental attitude; Indiana All-Star;
MVP and captain as a college senior at Northwestern;
Indiana Basketball Hall of Famer

Every few months, Mike Weaver, Bob Straight, and Bob Hammel—all Huntington products—meet for lunch and reminisce about their basketball careers, which earned each of them a place in the Indiana Basketball Hall of Fame—Weaver as a player, Straight as a coach and administrator, and Hammel as a sports writer.

"We talk about the same stuff every time we get together," said Weaver, an Indiana All-Star in 1964, and later an MVP and captain of the Northwestern University Wildcats his senior year. "The beautiful thing about getting older is that we forget, and therefore we tend to exaggerate a little bit more. I think the world of both of them. Coach Straight, next to my dad, had more influence on my life than any other man. Of course, Bob Hammel is such a gentleman and fun to be with. And we all three absolutely love basketball."

They usually break bread in Indianapolis, where the headquarters of the Weaver Popcorn Co. is located. Weaver is president. Straight, who won eight sectionals, four regionals, and one semistate as Vikings coach, still resides in Huntington. He is a past president of the Indiana Coaches

Association, and the IHSAA Board of Control. Hammel lives in Bloomington, where he served as sports editor of the *Bloomington Herald-Times* from 1966-96.

Weaver's love affair with basketball started early. After the Toledo, Ohio, native moved to Huntington with his family as a youngster, he finally was able to talk his conservative father into buying him a goal, and putting it on the garage. His father told him, "If you want a ball, you're going to have to go out and earn some money to buy your own ball."

Before he could earn enough money, Weaver met a young fellow who had a ball. He brought the ball, and the two played together in Weaver's backyard. Weaver was finally able to purchase his own ball after saving enough money shoveling snow. In the third grade he got to go into the big gym and shoot baskets. "I can remember having trouble going to sleep that night I was so excited," he said. "I had my own ball and I slept with it."

Of Straight as a coach, Weaver says, "He is a most outstanding human being, most importantly. He was a great teacher and a great coach, and he brought a discipline, an understanding of the game, and a strategy that we were introduced to at a young age, which was helpful."

Straight required the Vikings to participate in three sports. Weaver played football, basketball, and ran track, or as he puts it, "I lumbered through track. It was very good playing three sports in that it gave us a good dose of humility, because we participated in sports in which maybe we weren't quite as strong as in basketball."

At the end of his sixth-grade year, Weaver, who was the fastest kid and best athlete in the class, learned a personal lesson that made him a better person and teammate.

"A kid by the name of Mike Shumaker moved to Huntington," said Weaver. "He was smaller than I was, but he was faster and a much better athlete, and I didn't like the fact he was better than me. In the seventh grade, we went undefeated in football and basketball, and I started realizing, boy, it's great having a guy like Mike Shumaker as my friend and teammate, because it's more about the team and less about me."

Another tuning point in Weaver's life occurred when he was a freshman on the varsity basketball team. Straight would always hold a practice New Year's morning, which was a way of making sure everybody got home at a good time New Year's Eve.

"Our head football coach, Jerry Huntsman, was the assistant basketball coach," said Weaver. "He and Coach Straight could be pretty animated in practices. I was expected to guard Kent Paul, a senior who was an all-state quarterback and played freshman basketball at IU. It was me, a boy, guarding Kent, a man. In that practice, Coach Straight and Huntsman cut me absolutely no slack. Coach Straight had a system that if you made mistakes you'd have to run the bleachers at the end. I was still running the bleachers after everybody else had run them, showered, got dressed, and left. I was so angry, I thought, 'I'm gonna quit. This is unfair. I shouldn't have to guard Kent Paul.' And yet, I somehow stuck it out."

When Huntington reached the state finals Weaver's senior year, he saw Huntsman, who later became the head football coach at Indiana State, and said to him, "Do you remember January 1, my freshman year?" Huntsman threw his head back and Weaver quickly added, "You expected me to guard Kent Paul."

Huntsman laughed and said, "You never thought you could do it, did you?"

Weaver exclaimed, "God, I love you, Coach."

During Weaver's freshman year, Jim Seneff moved to Huntington and became an integral part of a team that became affectionately known as the "Clean Cuts." Weaver welcomed him with open arms.

"You look at Huntington County from the mid-'50s to the mid-'60s in terms of just a lot of things working really, really well," said Weaver, "and it was a very magical time. We were blessed to be a part of that. Our basketball team grew every year. I fully appreciated that when I went on to college, because I got into a situation where I didn't grow every year. What I learned is how important a teacher, a coach, or someone outside of yourself is to your growth, because Coach Straight absolutely expected, he demanded, improvement. The beauty of it was that we as teenagers thought we could be about this good, and our expectations of ourselves didn't even approach what Coach Straight's were."

Weaver and Shumaker, also an Indiana All-Star in 1964, advanced to the Fort Wayne semistate all four years as Vikings. They lost to Kokomo in the afternoon in 1961 and '62, then beat Noblesville in the afternoon in '63 before losing to South Bend Central in the championship game.

"That kinda whetted our appetite," said Weaver. In 1964, Huntington defeated Kokomo and Elkhart in the semistate to move to the state finals against Columbus, Lafayette Jeff and Evansville Rex Mundi. Weaver scored 22 points as the Vikings beat Columbus, 71-67, in the afternoon and Lafayette downed Rex Mundi, 74-61.

In the title game, won by Lafayette, 58-55, Weaver had only five points. "I'd love to play that one over," he said. "I wouldn't get three offensive fouls that quickly. That was a matter of not picking up on what they were doing. I didn't play very much, which was too bad, because it's every kid's dream to win the state championship."

Receiving the Trester Award "was very special," says Weaver. "It says something about the community of Huntington, my teachers, my minister, my coach, my parents."

Weaver dreamed of going to Indiana University. "If Bobby Knight had been at IU when I graduated and had I had an opportunity, I would have been there in a heartbeat," he said. "I went for a weekend, and stayed with Tom and Dick VanArsdale and Jon McGlocklin. Walking around campus with Tom and Dick was pretty impressive, but I didn't like Branch McCracken's style of basketball. Coach Straight was very disciplined, with a heavy emphasis on defense. Branch's style was quite the opposite. I wanted to focus on a more controlled type of game."

Weaver chose Northwestern over Duke and Michigan, because, according to *Sports Illustrated*, the Wildcats had the best recruiting class in the country the year before Weaver went there; the enrollment was relatively small (6,500); and he thought the coach Larry Glass, was a "super fine guy." Ironically, the Wildcats turned out to be more a Branch McCracken-type of team than a Bob Straight-type team, averaging over 92 points Weaver's junior season.

Northwestern scored 108 points in a home game against Kentucky, but lost, 110-108. "I can't tell you how many I scored, but I can tell you about the shot I missed at the end of the game," said Weaver. "A play was set for me, and I shot from the side of the free throw line. I could hit eight of 10 consistently, but not that night."

The Chicago Bulls of the NBA drafted Weaver in a lower round, and he believes he could have made the end of the bench for a season. "Now I wish I would have," he said. But there was no signing bonus offered, and the pay wasn't much for where a 6'4" forward was chosen, so Weaver opted to study for an MBA at Northwestern after serving two years in military service. He played a lot of basketball in Germany while in the Army.

Weaver's grandfather started the Weaver Popcorn Co. in 1928, and Weaver joined the company in 1972. He worked with his late father for 30 years. The popcorn factory, which supplies about 30 percent of the popcorn consumed throughout the world, is located in Van Buren, Indiana, and has about 450 associates, the name Weaver uses for his employees. They contribute a percentage of the company's pre-tax profits each year to the Weaver Popcorn Foundation, which goes toward scholarships.

Weaver has not met Indianapolis native Dave Letterman, but the television host contacted the company, and loves to eat a product called Explod-O-Pop. Weaver and his wife, Becky, are both married a second time. She has adopted twin sons, and he has a son and a daughter, both of whom work in the company business. The Weavers have five grandchildren.

"My wife loves to go to basketball games with me, and I still get butterflies when I go," said Weaver. "To the day I die, I'm gonna love basketball."

Dick Dickey

Pendleton High School, Pendleton

Year graduated
1944

Major accomplishments
All-sectional as a senior at Pendleton High; Indiana Basketball Hall of Famer

Fifty-nine years after Dick Dickey helped put a spark in the North Carolina State program, the Pendleton High School graduate was inducted into the Indiana Basketball Hall of Fame. Dickey's wife, Jean, and five of their eight children attended the induction ceremony on March 23, 2005, in Indianapolis. What made Dickey's night even more special was the appearance of Monte Towe, an instrumental player in N.C. State's 1974 NCAA championship, at the dinner.

"Monte knew I was going into the hall, but he surprised me by driving up from New Orleans with his wife to see the induction," said Dickey of Towe, whom he had recommended to Wolfpack coach Norm Sloan in 1971 after his friend had made the Indiana All-Star team. How Towe got to Raleigh, North Carolina, is an amusing story. Dickey, who died on July 3, 2006 at age 79, had tried to convince Sloan to offer 1967 Indiana All-Star John Mengelt of Elwood a scholarship.

"Norm got the N.C. State job late that year, and didn't have much time for recruiting," said Dickey. "I saw Mengelt almost beat Marion single-handedly in the Marion sectional. I told Norm he'd better go after Mengelt. Well, Norm didn't do anything." As a college senior at Auburn, Mengelt scored 45 points in a 95-91 victory at N.C. State. It is the highest total by an opposing player against the Wolfpack.

"Norm went up to Mengelt afterward and said, 'Dick Dickey tried to get me to take you. I just didn't follow through with it.'" Dickey said that after hearing Mengelt's reply, "Norm got sick."

Four years after missing on Mengelt, Sloan asked Dickey to look at a guard who was playing against Towe's Oak Hill team of Converse. Halfway through the second quarter, Dickey turned to his wife and said that he was looking at the wrong player. A short time later Dickey drove Sloan from Bloomington to Indianapolis. When Sloan asked him if he had found him a guard, Dickey said yes, but not the one Sloan had asked him to watch. Towe was the player he recommended.

Sloan asked how big Towe was. Dickey said 5-foot-7. Sloan said he couldn't take anybody that little, to which Dickey replied, "Look at the publicity you'd get, Norm. Tom Burleson's going to be 7-foot-4, and Monte Towe's 5-foot-7. That's natural publicity. Besides, Towe can play." Sloan acquiesced, saying, "Okay, tell him he's got a scholarship, 'cause I'm not having you holler at me four more years."

Every time Towe saw Dickey he insisted he owed him plenty for whatever success he's had since his high school days. Dickey always replied, "Not really, Monte. All I did was give you opportunity. You made it from there."

N.C. State was known as the Red Terror when Dickey joined Sloan and Pete Negley of Indianapolis, Charlie Stine of Frankfort, Jack McComas of Shelbyville, and Harold Snow of Anderson in Raleigh in the fall of 1946. On December 2, 1947, Case's team became known as the Wolfpack. Not only did his program have a new nickname, it had a new direction after going 57-72 in the previous seven seasons.

"Timing was everything," said the 6'1" Dickey, who played forward in college after being a guard who hadn't shot much on some poor Pendleton teams. "I was lucky. I got there at the right time, and people were ready for a change, you know being after World War II. We came in and started winning. And the fans took us in their hearts."

In Dickey's four seasons under Case, who coached Frankfort High School to four Indiana state championships, the Wolfpack had records of 26-5, 29-3, 25-8, and 27-6. The team went to two NIT tournaments in that span, and in 1950 they traveled to the NCAA Final Four in New York City.

N.C. State lost to CCNY (City College of New York), 78-73, in the semifinals, then defeated Baylor, 53-41, in a consolation game. CCNY won both the NCAA and NIT titles that year.

Dickey, who captained the 1949-50 team, is one of only three N.C. State players to earn All-America honors three times, and is the only four-time all-conference selection in school history. He led the Wolfpack to four successive Southern Conference titles (N.C. State went into the ACC in 1953). Dickey became the first Wolfpack player drafted by the NBA, Baltimore in 1950.

Instead of going to Baltimore, Dickey opted to play with the Anderson Packers, who had been members of the old National Basketball League, during the 1950-51 season. The Packers' league didn't last, so Dickey went to Baltimore in 1951, but soon was sold to the Celtics. He played behind Bob Cousy and Bill Sharman. Dickey's minutes and pay weren't excessive, so he decided to go to work after one season. He did continue to play independent ball until he was near 40 years old.

How good was Dickey? "The farther from it, the better I was," he said with a chuckle. "The players of my day didn't get to watch a lot of TV and film. I remember Norm Sloan calling me one day. He said he was looking at some old film, then added, 'Dick, you were a lot better than I thought you were.' I told him I thought that was a compliment."

Shortly after being named all-sectional for Pendleton as a senior in 1944, Dickey enlisted in the Navy. Three days after graduating, the 5'9", 150-pound 17-year-old went to Norman, Oklahoma, for training. "I hadn't grown up yet," he said.

From Norman, Dickey was sent to California for pre-flight training (he never did get a pilot license). Dickey played on a service basketball team that won 29 straight games. At the same time, Case was coaching a pre-flight team in Ottumwa, Iowa. The Navy decided to let the teams play for a championship, and Case's team won it with narrow victories in Iowa and in California.

Dickey must have impressed Case, because he got an invitation to join five other Hoosier hotshots in Raleigh after his two-year military service. He ended up going south instead of enrolling at Purdue on the G.I. Bill. Those hotshots changed southern basketball forever, and Dickey was in the forefront of the revolution. On February 25, 1947 the game between N.C. State and Duke was postponed when fire officials closed down Thompson gym in Raleigh the afternoon before the game. Fans had sneaked in through bathroom windows, broke down doors, and hid in the basement in an effort to see the game without purchasing tickets. The gym seated about 1,500, but more than double that would have been packed into the bleachers if the fire officials hadn't intervened.

"I think that was the start of basketball craziness down there," said Dickey, who was MVP in the first Dixie Classic held in December, 1949. Dickey also took part in starting the college tradition of cutting down nets after a tournament victory. Case had done that after winning Indiana high school tournaments, so he had his team do it after winning the Southern Conference tournament in 1947.

Dickey, who resided in Marion following his retirement in 1992 after a 30-year stint with Farm Bureau Insurance, returned to Raleigh in 1999 when his alma mater retired his No. 70 jersey. New Castle has a No. 70 Dickey jersey on display in the Indiana Basketball Hall of Fame.

"I don't know of any other high school hall of fame that would compare with that one," he said. "People [in the south] have told me they couldn't visualize it being that big of a draw, and how big basketball was in Indiana."

Monte Towe

Oak Hill High School, Converse

Year graduated
1971

Major accomplishments
Sank all 24 of his free throws in the sectional; Indiana All-Star;
Indiana Basketball Hall of Famer

M onte Towe remembers vividly the night he and his late father, Corwin, walked out of the Oak Hill High School gym after watching the Golden Eagles play a basketball game. Towe wasn't more than 4-foot-6 at the time.

"My father was always my greatest fan," said Towe, who returned to his alma mater, North Carolina State, as associate coach in the summer of 2006 after five years as the coach at the University of New Orleans. "He also was my biggest critic. I had just watched Earl Brown play for Oak Hill. He was 6-foot-7 and really good. He played at Purdue in the '60s. I said, 'Dad, am I ever going to be as tall as Earl Brown?' He said, 'No, but you can be as good.'"

Towe never came close to equaling Brown in height, but he may have accomplished more at a mere 5-foot-7 in football, basketball, and baseball than any other Indiana athlete. Indianapolis Lawrence North High School coach Jack Keefer, Towe's freshman coach at Oak Hill, was not surprised by Towe's feats.

"He's one mighty person," said Keefer. "Monte was kind of a Michael Jordan-type, a very competitive person. I remember a JV basketball game at Wabash when Monte was probably about 5-foot-4. You didn't win very often there, and we were behind. Monte started crying, and every time he crossed the 10-second line, he'd just shoot it and the ball would go in. We ended up winning. Soon afterward he went to the varsity."

Towe grew up in Converse, Indiana, the youngest of four children of Corwin and Frances Towe. "Converse was, and remains, a town of about 1,000 people," he said. "The excitement in Converse always seemed like it revolved around the fish fries, the church camps, and basketball—sports in general. If we weren't playing football, we were playing basketball; and if we weren't playing basketball, we were playing home run derby. I have a great brother and two great sisters who steered me in the right direction. It was a real positive environment to grow up in."

Knowing that you are going to be small can be a huge motivational tool, especially if you love sports the way Towe, who became known as "The Flea" in high school, does.

"I was always challenged," he said. "If you're standing around the playground as a young kid, the big guys usually get chosen first and the little guys last. It certainly made me aware that I was going to have to do something a little bit special to catch the attention of my coaches and the people I was going to have to impress."

One of the best pieces of advice Towe ever received came from one of his first coaches, Dave Huffman. He told Towe that he had to learn to get his shot off quickly because of his height; he also suggested shooting over a ladder during the summer. The ladder was almost 7 feet tall, and Towe was around four foot.

"All I did that summer was go home and shoot up over that ladder," Towe said. "I give credit to the guys who encouraged me to play, and who tried to help me. When I give clinics and talks, I always mention the name of my high school football coach, Jim Law, as being one of the greatest influences on me as far as a person, and as far as being an athlete." Law went into the Indiana Football Hall of Fame in 2005.

In Towe's sophomore and junior seasons, the Golden Eagles lost to Marion in the sectional. "We played against what has to be one of the best high school teams in Indiana never to win the state championship, that Marion team of 1969," he said. "It had Joe Sutter, Cutty Townsend, and Jovon Price. They lost to Indianapolis Washington in the afternoon of the state finals.

"We beat the Giants in Marion in front of about 6,000 people in one of the best wins ever for Oak Hill. We were a Milan-esque team from a really small town. We got beat by Elkhart in the semistate. What an exciting time for me and my teammates and the whole Oak Hill community, because both our football and basketball teams were outstanding."

Towe scored 96 points in three sectional games in 1971, and sank all 24 of his free throws. Dick Dickey, a Hoosier native who was one of coach Everett Case's first recruits at N.C. State in the 1940s, touted Towe to coach Norm Sloan of the Wolfpack. Dickey had found Towe when he went to scout Steve Ahlfeld of Northfield. It didn't take long to switch his attention to one of Northfield's opponents. Sloan, a teammate of Dickey's at State as well as a Hoosier native, became sold on Towe.

How did David Thompson, 6-foot-4, and Tom Burleson, 7-foot-4, react to seeing the 5-foot-7 Towe for the first time?

"They thought I was somebody's little brother," said Towe. "They'd heard that Coach Sloan had signed a little guy from Indiana. Nobody knew who I was. I don't think anybody expected me to do anything. But it seemed like from the day we first met we really meshed."

In Towe's sophomore season, the Wolfpack was on probation and couldn't play in the NCAA tournament. The team went 27-0. "I think the sanctions were way too harsh for whatever was out there," he said. "The only thing we could do was win every game we played."

The next season State went 30-1, its only loss being 84-66 early to UCLA and Bill Walton in St. Louis. "I think it motivated us to go on and have a great rest of the year," said Towe.

State was undefeated in the ACC regular season in Towe's sophomore and junior seasons, but had to win the 1974 ACC tournament to qualify for the NCAA tournament; at the time, only the conference champion made it to the tournament. State beat Maryland, 103-100, in overtime in what many observers believe was one of the best college games ever played.

"The pressure in that game was incredible," said Towe. "Now when you go to the ACC or Big Ten tournament there's five or six teams making the NCAA tournament. Maryland had a great team—John Lucas, Lenny Elmore, Tom McMillen; Lefty Driesell was their coach. It was probably the best individual game I've ever seen a guy play. Tommy Burleson was dominant with 38 points."

The Wolfpack defeated Providence, 92-78, and Pittsburgh, 100-72, to win the Eastern Regional at Raleigh, North Carolina, and earn a rematch with UCLA in the Final Four at Greensboro, North Carolina. State ended

UCLA's string of seven consecutive NCAA championships in the semifinal round, 80-77, in two overtimes.

"Being in Greensboro definitely had a positive effect on us," said Towe. "But we were motivated to win no matter where we played. UCLA was still good, and they were seven points ahead in the second overtime, but we were able to overcome that in the last two minutes. Obviously, John Wooden, their coach and a great champion, and Bill Walton, Keith Wilkes, and David Meyers made them a formidable opponent; but we were able to get a great win for the Wolfpack."

Sloan didn't allow the Wolfpack to have a letdown in the championship game, and State defeated Marquette, 76-64, to earn the school its first NCAA title. Towe had 16 points in that game, and was named all-tourney.

"After the game I just sat on the bench and soaked up the moment," he said. "I enjoyed the pinnacle of a college basketball player's career, winning a national championship."

A few months later the Wolfpack baseball team won the ACC tournament, and Towe and another Hoosier, Tim Stoddard, went to Omaha, Nebraska, for the College World Series. State was eliminated in two games.

"Tim and I were major players in basketball and baseball," said Towe. "Tim was a power forward in basketball, and he pitched 10 years in the major leagues. He has a World Series championship ring. Tim's also a great winner."

The NBA Atlanta Hawks drafted Towe, but coach Larry Brown of the Denver Nuggets in the ABA offered him a no-cut contract. Towe played the last year of the ABA and one year in the NBA. Denver lost to the New York Nets in the ABA championship series, and to eventual NBA champion Portland in the playoffs the following year.

"Even though maybe I wasn't nearly as important when I played in Denver as I was when I played at N.C. State, I still was very proud of the fact I was on a team that won a lot," said Towe.

The 2005-2006 college season was difficult for Towe and his team after Hurricane Katrina forced them to move to the University of Texas at Tyler. Of the disaster, he said, "I feel fortunate that we made it through Katrina without any deaths or other tragedies. I wish the storm had never hit, but the important thing is we were together as a team, and I'm together with my wife. I tell my players it's a matter of opportunity. I wouldn't have been able to be an NCAA champion without Dick Dickey and Norm Sloan. Even though he's dead, Norm still remains my favorite guy of all-time."

Ken Pennington

Warren Central High School, Indianapolis

Year graduated
1956

Major accomplishments
Made the Warren Central varsity team as a freshman; Ranks 24th on the Bulldogs' all-time scoring list with 1,117 points scored from 1957-1960; Played in three Hoosier Classics; Played in two NIT tournaments; Indiana Basketball Hall of Famer

Cameron Indoor Stadium on the campus of Duke University in Durham, North Carolina, was never a destination for Ken Pennington when he played for Butler University over 40 years ago. That changed in early 2005 when Pennington's grandson, Josh McRoberts, a senior at Carmel High School, said, "Papa, do you want to go with me to see Duke play North Carolina in the last game of the regular season? It's at Duke."

Pennington, a former high school coach at Mooresville, Rochester, and Rushville, said, "Absolutely." The two of them flew to Durham, where the 6-foot-10 McRoberts had become a prized recruit of Duke coach Mike Krzyzewski.

"I sure have become a Duke fan," said Pennington, who stands 24th on Butler's all-time leading scoring list, four spots below Josh's father, Tim McRoberts, who scored 1,208 points as a Bulldog from 1980-1984. "I've always been a Krzyzewski fan, just because I think he does things really well in a quiet, discreet way. I like his mannerisms. I like his professionalism."

The trip with his grandson provided Pennington his first chance to chat with Coach K. He told Pennington that he was happy to have Josh as a Blue Devil.

"I said, 'There are two things I'm concerned about. Josh does not shoot the ball well. If he could shoot, there would be no limit to what he can do.' And I said another thing is that in Josh's life, he has never been pushed to his physical limit. I said he's just been bigger than everybody and they haven't pushed him, and he hasn't worked hard.

"Coach K said, 'I'll tell you this. We will work with his shooting, and you won't believe the improvement on it in a year.' And he said, 'that second concern you never have to worry about it again.'"

Pennington, who was surprised how small and noisy Cameron Indoor Stadium is (it seats less than 10,000), said his grandson has reacted to his concerns in a positive way. "Josh says he's never worked as hard as he did in his first year at Duke, and I believe it. If you watch him play defense, he hustles down the floor like I've never seen him hustle down the floor in my life. I'm really impressed with the effort he's giving, and I know Coach K will make my grandson a better basketball player. I have no doubt about that."

Blackie Braden and Tony Hinkle were two coaches who made Pennington a better basketball player than he ever thought he could be. Braden was Pennington's coach at Warren Central before Blackie went to Indianapolis Southport High School after his Warriors team won the Marion County tournament in 1954. Hinkle became a legend as the Butler coach.

"The Bradens—Blackie and his lovely wife Barbara—took me under their wing when I was a very young kid," said Pennington. "We got Mr. Braden a better job by winning the county tournament I always told him. I was able to play as a freshman on the varsity at Warren Central, and I felt I had a pretty good career there playing for Bob Meyers after Mr. Braden went to Southport. Mr. Braden went to Butler, and he encouraged me to go there. It was the greatest thing that ever happened for me in terms of my future. Mr. Hinkle got me into coaching."

Pennington chuckles when he recalls how low-key Hinkle was about recruiting him. Braden set up an appointment for Pennington, who went by himself to see Hinkle. "Mr. Hinkle's famous words were, 'Whatever you can't do, kid, we'll do for you,'" said Pennington. "That was his offer of a full scholarship. He never called me 'Ken', it was always 'kiddo' or 'Warren Central.'"

In Pennington's estimation, the secret to Hinkle's success was that he was not only conservative as a coach, but he also was humble and conservative in his lifestyle. "He was a fundamentalist," said Pennington. "We did the same thing the last day of practice my senior year that we did the first day of practice when I was a freshman. It was so repetitive you really got bored or anxious, saying, 'Man, I'll be glad when this is over, because every day it's going to be the same thing.' He made me a better player through the repetition I did on a daily basis."

Seven-foot Mike McCoy, 1958 Mr. Basketball, can attest to what Hinkle did for Pennington. "I played against a guy in the summer leagues I had never heard of before," said McCoy. "The guy was named Ken Pennington. The first time I played against him he grabbed my left leg, held it, twirled around me, and went in for a lay-up. That caught me off guard. Even though he was 6'5", I could have blocked his shot; but the whole game this guy did things that just amazed me. I was talking to him later, and he said it was all Hinkle."

In Pennington's three varsity seasons under Hinkle, Butler was 14-20 in preseason play against the likes of Ohio State, Michigan State, Illinois, Wisconsin, Michigan, Indiana, Purdue, Notre Dame, Tennessee, UCLA, and Bradley.

"That was a tremendous opportunity to play against great teams and great players," said Pennington. "The best team I ever played against was in my senior year when we played Ohio State, who won the NCAA national championship that year. That was the year [Jerry] Lucas and [John] Havlicek and [Mel] Nowell, and [Larry] Siegfried, and [Joe] Roberts, and of course [Bob] Knight were on the Ohio State team. Knight, [who had led Indiana to NCAA titles in 1976, 1981, and 1987], didn't play any, but he was there. Their coach, Fred Taylor, was one of the nicest gentlemen I ever met in the coaching field."

How did Pennington do against the Buckeyes? "The first game [in Columbus] I did really well," he said. Butler won, 77-73, in overtime in the 1957-58 season. A year later Ohio State won, 81-69, in Hinkle Fieldhouse. In the 1959-60 season, the Buckeyes won, 99-66, at Columbus and 96-68. In my senior year Lucas guarded me at Ohio State, and I did pretty well. Then they played us back at Butler about a month later, and I didn't know there was a ball in the game. Havlicek guarded me, and he wouldn't even let me have the ball. I didn't get the ball until late in the game after they were probably 20 or 30 points ahead. I had a different feeling for defense and Havlicek after that game. He was an outstanding defensive player even in college, and went to the pros and did the same thing [for the Boston Celtics]."

Pennington played against Indiana and Purdue three years in the Hoosier Classic at Hinkle Fieldhouse before huge crowds. Notre Dame was the fourth team in the double-headers on successive nights. Butler was 3-3 in those three Hoosier Classics. The Bulldogs played in the National Invitation Tournament twice during Pennington's three seasons. They lost to St. John's, 76-69, in 1958; and to Bradley, 83-77, in 1959.

Pennington was born in Berea, Kentucky, and he loved the Wildcats. He became a Hoosier in the eighth grade when his father bought a trailer park on the east side of Indianapolis.

"Basketball was kinda in our family," said Pennington. "I had an older brother who went to Georgetown College on a basketball scholarship. My mother wouldn't let me play football. She said it was too rough for somebody like her baby boy. I was very interested in basketball and the Wildcats, then we moved to Indianapolis and Blackie Braden took me in."

Pennington received letters from the Los Angeles Lakers and Cincinnati Royals of the NBA asking him to try out, but he knew he couldn't play in the middle at 6'5", and he wasn't a good enough ball-handler to play outside, so he went another direction.

"I really wanted to coach," said Pennington, who retired in 2000 after spending 13 years as a coach and administrator, and the last 11 years as the Pike Township transportation director in Indianapolis. "I thought, 'You know, I can start out at $6,000 a year and man, I'll really be wealthy."

Pennington owns a 452-acre farm near Frankfort, Kentucky. He and his second wife, Mary, spend summers there or in Indianapolis, where they have a condo. In 2005 they purchased a condo in Bonita Springs, Florida.

Pennington says Josh only gets four tickets for games in Cameron Indoor Stadium. Jennifer McRoberts, Josh's mother, and his grandmother Carolyn, Pennington's first wife, made good use of those tickets in Josh's freshman season. They rented a condo in Durham, and often spent several days there when the Blue Devils played mid-week and on Saturdays at home.

Papa didn't miss any of his grandson's action in the 2005-2006 season. "Having somebody to follow at this time in my life has inspired me. Every game that Duke played in the regular season was on some form of TV: CBS, NBC, ESPN, Fox. I was in Florida, and you know at my age I really enjoy sitting right here in the sunny South watching those games."

ABOVE: From inside or outside, Lebanon's Rick Mount could always score, as "The Rocket" shows on this layup attempt. Photo courtesy of Indiana Basketball Hall of Fame

RIGHT: Indianapolis Washington's George McGinnis put up some awesome numbers in the second All-Star game of 1969–53 points and 31 rebounds. Photo courtesy of Indiana Basketball Hall of Fame

LEFT:
"The Miracle Man,"
Clay City's Bob
Heaton, makes the
left-handed shot that
sent Indiana State to
the famous 1979 NCAA
Final Four.
Photo courtesy of Indiana State
University Archives Athletic
Photograph Collection

RIGHT:
Before Carl Erskine
began throwing
strikes for the Brooklyn
Dodgers, he threw
beautiful passes
to Anderson High
teammate "Jumpin'"
Johnny Wilson as a
5-foot-9 guard.
Photo courtesy of Carl Erskine

Bill (right) and Dave Shepherd (below) of Carmel are the only brothers ever to wear the No. 1 Mr. Basketball jersey in different years—Billy in 1968, Dave in 1970.

Photos courtesy of Dave Shepherd

LEFT:
After Mike Warren helped Hoosiers native John Wooden in two of his record 10 NCAA titles at UCLA, the South Bend Central product's coach said Warren was the smartest player he had ever coached.
Photo courtesy of Indiana Basketball Hall of Fame

RIGHT:
Twins Arley (34) and Harley Andrews teamed with their uncle, Harold Andrews, on the 1953 Terre Haute Gerstmeyer team in forming one of the most famous family combinations in Indiana high school basketball history.
Photo courtesy of Harley Andrews

RIGHT:
Although he was just 6-foot-2 as Indianapolis Washington's center when the Continentals won the 1965 state championship, Ralph Taylor was never outrebounded that season.
Photo courtesy of Ralph Taylor

LEFT:
Not only did 7-foot Eric Montross help Indianapolis Lawrence North win the 1989 state championship and become an All-Star in 1990, he was an NCAA champion with North Carolina in 1993.
Photo courtesy of Lawrence North High School

LEFT:
At 5-foot-7, Monte Towe (shooting) was called "The Flea" while at Oak Hill High in Converse; then he became known as the "Little Big Man" while helping North Carolina State win the 1974 NCAA championship.
Photo courtesy of Oak Hill High School

RIGHT:
Chuck DeVoe became the first of three brothers from Indianapolis Park School to play basketball and tennis at Princeton, where he won the Bunn Trophy as the Tigers' basketball MVP as a senior in 1952.
Photo courtesy of Chuck DeVoe

Ron Bonham, nicknamed the "Blond Bomber," had plenty of practice cutting down nets as a product of Muncie Central and the University of Cincinnati.
Photo courtesy of Ron Bonham

RIGHT:
Huntington's Mike Weaver accepts the Trester Award after the Vikings, who were known as the "Clean Cuts," lost to Lafayette Jeff in the 1964 state championship game.
Photo courtesy of Indiana Basketball Hall of Fame

LEFT:
After leading Evansville North to the 1967 state championship, Bob Ford moved on to Purdue where he scored often for the Boilermakers in Mackey Arena.
Photo courtesy of Indiana Basketball Hall of Fame

Bob Ford

Evansville North High School, Evansville

Year graduated
1968

Major accomplishments
Scored a record 128 points in the final four games of the 1967 state tournament; Indiana All-Star; Indiana Basketball Hall of Famer

There were no *Hoosiers* moments for Bob Ford and his Evansville North teammates when they arrived at Hinkle Fieldhouse in Indianapolis in 1967 for the Indiana high school basketball tournament finals. However, in the next 48 hours Ford, who scored a record 128 points in the final four games of the tournament, which was later broken by George McGinnis in 1969 with 148 points, would learn the true meaning of Hoosier Hysteria.

Ford had never seen a state finals game in person; he had always watched on television. He said, "To walk into that building after seeing it on television and all the stuff that's written about the state tournament, it's an awe-inspiring moment. We had seen some big crowds in Evansville, because we played in Roberts Stadium. We saw 10,000 to 12,000 people for sectional, regional, and semistate. But [Hinkle Fieldhouse] with all its history was totally different."

In the afternoon round, North defeated New Castle, 66-56; and Lafayette beat Fort Wayne South, 79-70. Before a capacity crowd of 14,983, North outlasted Lafayette, 60-58. Ford had 35 points against New Castle, and followed up with 27 in the championship game.

"We had two state trooper cars leading our bus back to Evansville the next day," said the 6-foot-7 Ford. "For some reason people knew the route we were taking, and there were an awful lot of congratulatory signs along the way. We stopped about an hour after we left Indianapolis to get something to eat. Then as many of us as could piled into the two state trooper cars. We ran the siren so hard it was dead by the time we got to Evansville."

The team climbed on a big ladder truck and rode through town. "Then we went to Roberts Stadium for a reception," said Ford. "We had about 12,000 people there. It was really neat, and that's what Hoosier Hysteria is all about."

Ford's scintillating performance in the finals, in which he had 25 field goals and 12 free throws for 62 points, earned him a spot on the late Tony Hinkle's all-time Indiana high school basketball "dream team." The former Butler University coach announced his selections in April, 1982: Ford; Fuzzy Vandivier, Franklin; Bobby Plump, Milan; John Townsend, Indianapolis Tech; McGinnis; Willie Gardner, Indianapolis Crispus Attucks; Oscar Robertson, Indianapolis Crispus Attucks; Homer Stonebraker, Wingate; Jim Bradley, East Chicago Roosevelt; and John Wooden, Martinsville.

"That was really an honor," said Ford. "There were some good players on there who played a lot of basketball. And being put in the hall of fame is probably the greatest honor you can have in the state of Indiana as an athlete."

Ford, who was born in Evansville on January 26, 1950, was an only child. He didn't know his father. When he was about eight, his mother remarried and he gained a stepbrother, Randy Wilkinson.

Of his new brother Randy, Ford says, "he was kind of a basketball nut. He loved to play on the weekends. He wasn't terribly tall, but had a lot of skill. He got me hooked on the sport, because I was big and tall, and kind of awkward at that point. But he helped me out with learning the game and the fundamentals and that sort of thing."

Randy and Ford bent curtain rods into the form of a rim, and used sheer curtains as a net. They built a little backboard, hung it in the garage, and shot tennis balls into their homemade basket.

"If you can put a tennis ball in a basket that size, a basketball into a hoop is not bad at all," said Ford.

Ford tried out for his eighth grade team, but was cut. He played intramural basketball for three weeks, until the eighth grade coach asked Ford to join the team, "because you're not learning anything in intramurals."

After playing junior varsity ball the first semester of his freshman year at North, Ford was elevated to the varsity, where he remained through '68 when he was named high school All-American. In the 1966-67 season, for the first time North won at all four levels of the tournament—sectional, regional, semi-state, and state.

"There probably were four or five teams in Evansville that could have gone all the way to state that year," said Ford. "It was just a matter of who got out of sectional. We were the fortunate ones."

Coach Jim Rausch had installed the Tennessee offense used by coach Ray Mears that season, and Ford says "it fit everybody on the club like a glove, working equally well against a zone as it did against a man-to-man defense.

"I had a team that somewhere in the middle of the year got the feeling that if we were going to go anywhere, and the coaches did this, that most of the offense had to come through me as center, either as a passer or a scorer. The other guys really caught onto that. As it turned out everybody got a chance to score quite a bit, because the defenses would pack the inside. When I caught the ball, the defense would collapse and that gave me opportunity to pass out to the guards or forwards to take a wing shot."

Steve Holland was North's point guard. He had 35 points in the state finals. Preston Smith, a strong defensive player, was the other guard. Jim Hildebrandt and Ron Jesop were the forwards. "Ron played down on the baseline and was a football player, first and foremost, so his bulk and strength inside really helped out," said Ford.

North lost to Evansville Reitz in the sectional championship game in Ford's senior year. The Indiana All-Stars lost twice to Kentucky in 1968. "Was it my best experience as a player in terms of playing, probably not," Ford said. "But it was very enjoyable playing with the other kids from around Indiana. If you remember, the game in Indianapolis never finished. There was a riot towards the end of the game. There were problems with the officiating, and some of the fans got out of control."

Ford says he had bushel-baskets full of letters from colleges seeking his services. He narrowed his choices to Indiana, Purdue, Kentucky, and Tennessee. "I think it was probably the coaches more than anything else that convinced me to be a Boilermaker. I liked the players who were there, and of course, Rick Mount was there during that time. It seemed Purdue was the right fit, not only athletically, but academically. In high school, I had been involved in music, and at Purdue I sang in the glee club all four years. I traveled with the glee club when I wasn't playing basketball."

Ford wasn't eligible as a freshman, but he did get to see the Boilermakers lose to UCLA in the championship game of the 1969 NCAA tournament at Louisville. "Our seats were, well, you couldn't have been any higher; but we were in the building, and that was all that was important."

Ford did not get to play in an NCAA tournament. In those days, teams had to win the Big Ten season title to make it. "We were in the hunt my sophomore year," he said. "We were not too bad my junior year, but in my senior year we were awful. We ended up 12-12 that year." Purdue lost to St. Bonaventure, 94-79, in the NIT in Ford's junior year.

Despite not making it to the NCAA tournament, Ford calls his Purdue career "everything I hoped it would be. I got a good education, and I saw tons of the country through our travels as a team. In the summer of 1970 I participated in the World University Games in Italy. We came in second to Russia, so we got a silver medal. In 1971, we played in Cali, Columbia, in the Pan American Games. Unfortunately, we were the first American team not to make the medal round."

Dave DeBusschere and Bill Bradley were the starting forwards for the New York Knicks of the NBA when Ford was drafted, so he opted to sign with the Memphis Tams of the ABA. He played nine games and averaged 1.6 points before being cut in December, 1972.

"I had my shot at it," said Ford. "When you get to that level, you find out pretty quick what your limitations are. I was challenged height-wise and quickness-wise."

It was about at that time that Ford began doing color commentary on television for Purdue games, a task that he still relishes. "I'm sure there are some of the alumni who have been watching games in Mackey Arena a lot longer than I have," he said. "I haven't missed very many, though. I enjoy the basketball and staying close to those young people."

After being released by the Tams, Ford made a quick move to the TV business. His first job was in sales for Channel 18 in Lafayette. After a year he moved to the Olympic Broadcasting Co. in Chicago as executive producer of its two sports franchises; the Chicago Bulls of the NBA, and the Chicago Cougars of the World Hockey Association. He was there six years. For the next 20 years Ford was in operations and programming for Lafayette TV station WLFI. In 2005, he became director of distribution for Farm Journal Electronic Media in Lafayette.

Ford and his wife, Paula, have three grown children: Rob, 28; Andrew, 23; and Kara, a sophomore at Purdue. Andrew was a walk-on basketball player at Purdue and received a scholarship in his senior season.

If his mother hadn't remarried, Ford admits his life "might have been totally different. Without my basketball experience, both in high school and college, I wouldn't be where I am today. It taught me about life, hard work, dedication, determination, all those good things."

Roger Burkman

Franklin Central High School, Indianapolis

Year graduated
1977

Major accomplishments
Averaged 21.3 points and 13 rebounds as a junior at Franklin Central, and
27.2 points and 12.5 rebounds as a senior; Dubbed
"instant defense" by the late Al McGuire as a color analyst for NBC

After averaging 27.2 points a game in the 1976-77 season as a senior at Franklin Central High School in southern Marion County, Roger Burkman went to the University of Louisville where he became known as the player who provided the Cardinals with instant defense during their march to the 1980 NCAA championship at Indianapolis in Market Square Arena.

"Al McGuire gave me the nickname 'instant defense' on national TV and it stuck," said Burkman, who became the athletic director in 2005 at Spalding University, a National Association of Intercollegiate Athletics school in Louisville. The late Al McGuire loved to immortalize players with signature nicknames.

"I didn't score a lot of points in college," said Burkman, who chose Louisville after spending a weekend with coach Denny Crum and his recruiting assistant, Bill Olsen, fishing, riding mini-bikes, and water skiing on the Ohio River. "Basically I was one of those guys who'd score off a steal, a rebound, or fast-break situation. I didn't necessarily pull up and shoot the ball much, because you've gotta remember, there were a lot of guys on our team that could score [like Darrell Griffith, Derek Smith, Wiley Brown, and Rodney McCray]."

Burkman didn't start a game in the magical season when the Cardinals went 33-3, and defeated Iowa, 80-72; and UCLA, 59-54, in the Final Four to earn Louisville its first NCAA title. He averaged just 3.9 points in 17.7 minutes a game. But his worth was far more telling in the little things he did when he came off the bench.

"Coach Crum had talked to me and said, 'Look, I've gotta have a coach on the floor,'" said Burkman. "It's somebody who's going to keep those guys in the game happy, and make sure they're where they're supposed to be in the offense, and distributing the ball to them. I had to sacrifice that part, not that I couldn't score. In fact, there were certain games I got the ball to score, because I was such a good free throw shooter. The bottom line is the reason I didn't score in college is because I didn't shoot the ball. Sometimes I might shoot two or three times a game. That's the role that [Crum] wanted me to play."

Burkman's worth was never more evident than in the Cardinals' 86-66 victory over top-seeded LSU in the Midwest Regional championship game at Houston that sent his team to the Final Four. He played 26 minutes, had eight points, seven assists, and only one turnover.

"When we went out to warm up, there was a whole section of LSU students, I think mostly football players, sitting at our end of the floor," said Burkman. "They called us 'Wildcat rejects.' Wildcats, of course, is the nickname for the University of Kentucky. Boy, those were fightin' words. I actually felt like sending those LSU students a thank you card, because that was real motivation for us."

"And Jim got a bath after that game," continued Burkman, referring to Jim Terhune, who covered the Cardinals for the *Louisville Times*. Terhune had picked LSU to beat Louisville, and his "prize" was to be thrown in the shower by the Cardinal players.

"You've gotta remember, Jim traveled with us all year," said Burkman. "He was like one of the gang."

Burkman remembers that he had to "beg, borrow and steal" about 20 tickets for the Final Four for his high school coach Norm Starkey, parents, brother Bill, and other family members along with some friends.

That championship was "the pinnacle of my career," says Burkman, and he remains immensely proud of his Al McGuire-inspired nickname.

"The fans knew that once I stepped on the floor that something was going to happen. We were going to pick the tempo up defensively and get after people."

Burkman, 48, who lived in Acton, Indiana, while growing up, was born at St. Francis Hospital in Beech Grove, Indiana, "in the heart of Hoosier Hysteria." Burkman's basketball career started early when his father, Elvin, and older brother, Bill, cut the center out of an old tire rim and nailed it to the side of the garage. Burkman began to shoot at the tire rim at about age four with a volleyball or kickball.

"It was a typical old garage painted white," said Burkman, "and as I grew, I was introduced to the wall when I played my brother, 'cause he'd smash me into it. I'd be covered by white paint a lot. Having Bill kind of tutoring me through the years, and playing with him and some of his friends made me a lot tougher; made me a better player."

Burkman played freshman and junior varsity basketball his first season at Franklin Central. In the summer before his sophomore season, Burkman played one-on-one against a Flashes player who had just graduated and was going to Purdue. Unbeknownst to Burkman, coach Starkey was watching.

"It was a battle, and I ended up winning," said Burkman. "When the season rolled around, I was thinking I would just be a jayvee player. Coach Starkey said, 'You're going to be a varsity player, son.'"

As a junior, Burkman averaged 21.3 points and 13 rebounds. His senior totals were 27.2 and 12.5. Burkman was the state's leading scorer for a while that season, but did not make the Indiana All-Star team. The Flashes lost to Indianapolis Marshall, which produced David "Pancho" Wright, a teammate of Burkman's at Louisville who became known for instant offense in 1979-80, in the sectional. That might have hurt his All-Star chances.

"That was probably the biggest disappointment in my career," said Burkman. "But you know what? Things happen for a reason. From the moment I was born, God blessed me with a great family, great parents and my teachers and coaches through the years. I couldn't ask for anything better."

During the season Wright uttered the following phrase that came true, even though at the time it seemed just wishful thinking: "The Ville is going to the Nap," meaning Louisville is going to Indianapolis for the Final Four. Burkman says he had more college offers "than you might think. There were tons and tons of little schools." He also was recruited by Purdue, Indiana,

Louisville, Evansville, and Wyoming, in addition to receiving calls from UCLA and Hawaii, but they were too far from home.

"I thought all along my senior year that I was going to go to Purdue," said the 6'5" Burkman. But Louisville came on really strong. Burkman had been recommended to the Louisville coaching staff by Rudy Mueller of Indianapolis, a Cardinal alum who had seen Burkman play well in a losing effort as a high school sophomore. Mueller introduced himself to Burkman, who had his head down, and said, "Son, keep your head up. You've got a bright future." The next thing Burkman knew Louisville was recruiting him.

After his senior season at Louisville, Burkman scored well in several all-star games and was picked by the Chicago Bulls in the sixth round of the NBA draft. He did well enough in preseason games to make the squad, but learned he had been waived after playing in just six games and scoring five points (all free throws) while listening to the radio following a Christmas shopping trip.

"Once the season started, I didn't get a chance to play," he said. "You know why? Guaranteed contracts. I didn't have one." Burkman finished the season playing for the CBA team in Anchorage, Alaska.

The Indiana Pacers invited Burkman to try out, and he thought he was going to Los Angeles for summer league competition. Unfortunately, the trip was canceled due to a budget cut, so Burkman took a position as a grad assistant on Crum's staff. He remained on the staff a year, before joining the sales staff of Pepsi-Cola in Louisville—a position that he held for six years. For the next ten years, Burkman worked in development for DeSales and Trinity high schools in Louisville.

Of his position at Spalding University, Burkman says, "I really enjoy the administrative end of athletics. We're a very strong academic school and we're hoping to move to NCAA Division III. Basketball has been a tool that God provided me, and I've used it to get an education and to meet a lot of nice people. And you better believe that I am a Louisville Cardinal season-ticket holder."

Pete Trgovich

East Chicago Washington, East Chicago

Year graduated
1971

Major accomplishments
**Indiana All-Star; Led all scorers in the final four games of the 1971
state tournament with 116 points**

W hen Pete Trgovich (pronounced TUR-go-vich) arrived at UCLA
to play college basketball for Indiana native John Wooden,
Californians were saying, "Man, we heard you scored 68 points in
one game."

To which Trgovich replied, "No, no, no. It was one day. I had 40 in the
afternoon, 28 at night. In California they all talked about the Indiana high
school tournament when it was just one winner. Now with class basketball,
there's nothing to talk about anymore."

The 1969-70 and 1970-71 seasons were magical for The Region, the
northwest sector of Indiana where East Chicago is located. East Chicago
Roosevelt won the 1970 state championship with a 28-0 record. Washington
followed with an equally scintillating season 29-0.

In the middle of the 1969-70 season, Roosevelt was ranked No. 1 and
Washington No. 3 when they met. "The papers billed it as the game of the
decade," recalled Trgovich, who became the head basketball coach at East
Chicago Central in 2005. "Roosevelt beat us by 23. Other than Bill Walton,
I've never played with or against anybody more dominant than Jim Bradley
of that Roosevelt team. I don't think the people in East Chicago or in the
state of Indiana really appreciate what a talent he was."

Roosevelt defeated Washington by just three points in the East Chicago sectional final, a game Trgovich believes the Senators should have won. From that game a seed was planted for Trgovich and his teammates.

"Roosevelt was the one that set the bar so high for us," said Trgovich. "They went undefeated and won the state championship. We figured we were going to do the same thing, which is kind of ridiculous when you think about it, having that goal and fulfilling it.

"Athletically, that was probably the best year of my life. I'll never forget, another student at the high school said to me, 'In the championship pictures you look so sad. What were you sad about?' I said, 'I just realized the year was all over.'"

That season ended on March 20, when the Senators defeated Floyd Central with a record one-game total in a 102-88 victory in the afternoon session at Hinkle Fieldhouse; and Elkhart, 70-60, in the championship game. Trgovich—who led all scorers in the final four tournament games with 116 points—had 40 points against Floyd Central's Superhicks, and 28 at night.

"The Superhicks made me a fan," said Trgovich. "Jerry Hale, their star player, went on to play at the University of Kentucky. We had a lead going into the fourth quarter, and I was guarding Hale. I held him to 12 points in the first three quarters. At the start of the fourth quarter he took me to the baseline and hit a sky hook. I just looked over at the bench with my palms up saying, 'Ain't nothing else I could do.' Hale ended up with 26 points, so he took it to me in the fourth quarter."

The 1971 Senators of coach John Molodet were ranked No. 1 all season. They scored 100 or more points in eight games, and became the third successive unbeaten state champion. Trgovich's Senators are considered one of the best teams ever in Indiana.

"There's no way of knowing which team was really the best," said Trgovich. "I don't know who did it, or how they got it, but there was a poll of the greatest high school basketballs teams of all time in the country. They put us at No. 17, which, just being in the top 25, is a huge compliment.

"The team they put in front of us from Indiana was Crispus Attucks of 1955, Oscar Robertson's junior year. It was comical, because the only thing I cared about was we were ahead of this team from San Diego that featured a 7-foot center named Bill Walton. They were 25th."

Trgovich narrowed his college choices to UCLA, Notre Dame, Kansas, and North Carolina State. He visited each school; however, Notre Dame was No. 1 on his list, because it was close to home and it was a Catholic school. But a funny thing happened on the way to wearing an Irish uniform.

"When I made my official visit, Johnny Dee was the coach," said Trgovich." He resigned maybe two minutes before I walked into the coach's office. Gene Sullivan was Dee's assistant and had he got the job, I still would have gone to Notre Dame. Digger Phelps came in, and basically he didn't want me. And I didn't care for him."

ESPN had not come onto the college basketball scene yet, and UCLA was about the only team Trgovich saw on television. "Look how lucky of a kid I was to have these choices. Had I been a little more mature, let somebody walk me through it a little better, maybe I wouldn't have chosen UCLA. Kansas is the most storied program in the history of basketball. I wasn't aware of that at the time. UCLA was the thing, and I wanted to be on a winner, and that's basically how I made my decision."

Trgovich got two championship rings as a Bruin, in his sophomore and senior seasons, but he says his career at UCLA was "real frustrating." Freshmen weren't eligible his first season, and he was homesick much of time. Trgovich feels he earned a starting guard spot as a sophomore, but Wooden preferred to go with a senior.

"I was sixth man for maybe half the year, then my minutes dropped," Trgovich said. "I was immature, and I didn't want to accept that, and I showed an attitude." But the team did claim Wooden's ninth national title and seventh in a row.

Trgovich says "Coach Wooden always said, 'It takes me a long time to determine my starting lineup, but once I decide, it takes me an equally long time to change my mind.'" Trgovich didn't start again as a junior, but Wooden changed his mind on his lineup the fourth game of the season in St. Louis, and started Trgovich against N.C. State. The Bruins won by 18 points.

N.C. State ended UCLA's NCAA winning streak in '74 by beating the Bruins in double overtime in the first round of the Final Four. The Wolfpack went on to win the championship. UCLA beat Kansas for third place, so Trgovich played against two of the schools he had considered attending.

After Trgovich had a slow start his senior season, Wooden thought about replacing him in the lineup. "Had that happened, it would have killed me," said Trgovich. He redeemed himself in the next game. He guarded the leading scorer in the country, and outplayed him. "The reason I did so well in that game is because I no longer had any pressure on me," said Trgovich. "From that point on I played very, very well."

The highlight of Trgovich's UCLA career came in the final conference game of the season against Southern Cal at the Sports Arena. The Bruins had to win that game to make the NCAA tournament, because at that time only the conference champion was eligible.

"The score was tied and USC had the ball," Trgovich said. "We took a timeout, and I told Coach Wooden, 'If I steal the ball, what do you want me to do?' He looked at me like I was crazy. I said, 'Coach, do you want me to push it up, or do you want me to call time out?' He said, 'Push it up.' It was like I was predicting another steal. I had stolen the ball the week before against California to win a game. USC was running a little weave. I gambled and left my man, and sure enough, I stole the ball. They fouled me, and after a time out or two, I sank both free throws and we won the game."

In the Final Four at San Diego, UCLA defeated Louisville, 75-74, in overtime; and Kentucky, 92-85, in the championship game.

"If you were an Indiana kid, who would you want to play for the national championship?—Kentucky," said Trgovich. "I got to guard the Mr. Basketball of Kentucky my senior year in high school, Jimmy Dan Connor. The other guard was the Mr. Basketball, Mike Flynn, of Indiana who beat me out my senior year in high school. Jerry Hale was on the Kentucky team, but couldn't get off the bench because of Connor and Flynn. I scored 14 points in the first half, and only ended up with 16. But I had a really great run in the tournament, and my career ended almost in story-book fashion."

Trgovich was drafted by San Diego of the ABA, and Detroit of the NBA. San Diego folded before the start of the 1975-76 season. Trgovich didn't go to the Pistons camp. "It was the biggest mistake of my life," he said. Trgovich did play one year of minor league basketball with the Rochester, New York, Zeniths, and had a special teammate—Jim Bradley.

Trgovich and his wife, Helen, live in Munster, Indiana. They have a son named Pete, who went to Marian College in Indianapolis in 2005 on a basketball scholarship, and helped the Knights win a conference title in tennis. They also have a daughter, Alaina, who is a senior at Munster High School, and is a nationally ranked tennis player.

Trgovich, who left his supervisor's job with Inland Steel because he hated it, has coached basketball at Purdue-Calumet in Hammond, South

Suburban Junior College in Chicago, and at Andrean High School in Gary before taking over the Cardinals in his hometown. His East Chicago Central High team won a sectional championship in his first season as coach. The team lost in the regional.

"I started coaching at too old of an age," he said. "To be honest, I never thought I would coach again, and I'm back in it, and I've had so much fun. Looking back I wish I hadn't put so much emphasis on the sport, but what happened to me was that I became one of the luckiest guys in the world—that here was a sport that I love so much, and I ended up having a son that loves it just as much as I do. I'm able to look at him and, through his eyes, see my life all over again."

Steve Welmer

Columbus High School, Columbus

Year graduated
1968

Major accomplishments
A starter in football, basketball, and baseball as a junior and senior at
Columbus; Scored 1,059 points as a Purple Ace in three varsity
seasons; Set a school record for field-goal percentage of .589;
Indiana Basketball Hall of Famer

One of the questions most frequently asked of Steve Welmer—a
former Columbus Bulldog center, and current premier NCAA
Division I basketball official—is how is he able to stand people
screaming at him while he referees a game.

"I'm going to tell you something," said Welmer, who now has the
largest schedule of any major college referee, working some 110 games a
season. "Back when we played in Evansville, and we were a Division II
national powerhouse and we went on the road, believe me there's nothing
people can yell at me now that I haven't heard before.

"We wore T-shirts instead of jerseys, and we wore those [warm-up]
robes. It seems like everywhere we went to play there were sellouts, because
everybody wanted to see the Purple Aces come in. We were so much
different wearing T-shirts and robes. They used to make fun of us."

Welmer still sees sellouts crowds as he performs in nine different
Division I conferences, and, of course, he still hears fans screaming at him;
but he loves what he does, and continues to prepare diligently while he
works full-time during the season.

"This is big money now we're talking about, not only in March Madness and the NCAA tournament, coaches contracts, and what they're paying referees," said Welmer. "There are probably 50 of us where it's become a fulltime job [at the Division I elite level]. I've been full time since 1993.

"For people who think we all of a sudden put a striped shirt on November 1, put a whistle around our neck, and all of a sudden start thinking about basketball, they don't have any idea of what goes on behind the scenes in the off-season as far as training, watching films, staying in shape, seminars, how much time we veterans spend at camps trying to teach younger guys to someday take our place when our time comes to retire. It's a big, big business."

Welmer and his wife, Linda, have three grown daughters and live in Bradenton, Florida. He moved there for the balmier weather so he could run, ride his bicycle, and play golf to stay in shape. Linda, who is retired from Northwest Airlines, acts as Welmer's secretary handling his travel plans, rental cars, and hotel reservations. Since Linda has flying privileges with Northwest, she will sometimes fly to where Welmer is located so that the couple can spend a few days together.

"I'll log almost half a million miles [in a season]," he said. "Even if I'm not refereeing the next day, then I'm on a plane going to another game or coming back home to Bradenton. Basically, I'll be on a plane for about 135 days in a row."

Although Welmer had no idea he'd wind up being full time when he first started refereeing some 32 years ago at Indiana high school games, he had excellent teachers of the game at home—Columbus High and the University of Evansville.

"I don't know how an athlete could be any more fortunate than I am to have played for three different hall of fame-type people," said Welmer. "My father, Robert, who played at Columbus High and the University of Cincinnati, is in the Indiana Basketball Hall of Fame; and I got to play for one of the all-time great high school coaches—not just in Indiana, but anywhere—Bill Stearman, who is in the Indiana Hall of Fame. Then I go down to Evansville and play for one of the all-time great college coaches, Arad McCutchan, who is in the National Hall of Fame. And my younger brother, David, who played at Ball State, was on the IHSAA Silver Anniversary team of 2000."

As a Bulldog, Welmer was a starter in football, basketball, and baseball in his junior and senior seasons. He was a center and defensive end in football. "I hiked for extra points and punts, too, so I did a little bit of everything," he said. Welmer was a first baseman in baseball.

"I was only 6-foot-7 my senior year in high school," said Welmer. "In my freshman, sophomore, and junior years at Evansville I grew an additional inch each year, so I got to be right at 6-foot-10. I think I've shrunk a little. I think I'm probably 6-foot-9 now."

The Bulldogs of 1967-68 were ranked No. 1 in the state 12 of 18 weeks, and averaged 92.3 points a game while finishing 23-3. That last loss was to Indianapolis Shortridge, 88-77, in the semistate.

"Even though there had been some great teams and players to come out of Columbus, we thought we had the best chance to get Bill Stearman his first state championship," said Welmer, who averaged 17.9 points and 13.7 rebounds that season. "So we were very disappointed it didn't happen. Shortridge was very good, but we thought we had the best team in Indiana."

Welmer had full basketball scholarship offers from Northwestern, Kent State, and Evansville, and a half-basketball, half-baseball scholarship offer from Arizona State. Even though Evansville was Division II then, he chose the Purple Aces because he wanted his parents to be able to see him play and because Stearman said he had never had anyone play for McCutchan, and "it would be awful nice" if he did go there.

"Back then Evansville was playing in the Indiana Collegiate Conference against Indiana State, Ball State, Valparaiso, St. Joe, and Butler, so I decided to go to Evansville," said Welmer. "I don't think my mom and dad missed a game in my college career.

"And I had a pretty good running mate. I played center, and a guy named Don Buse, who played 13 years as a professional guard, and I were roommates. He and I are still the best of friends. I'll tell you how good Evansville was when Jerry Sloan and Larry Humes played there in 1965. That was the year when UCLA and Gail Goodrich were Division I national champions. Many people say that Evansville might have been the best in the country that season, bar none."

Welmer averaged 29.7 as a freshman for the Purple Aces (freshmen weren't eligible for the varsity then). He scored 1,059 points in three varsity seasons and set a school record for field-goal percentage of .589.

After graduation in 1972, Welmer moved to Indianapolis and became a field sales rep trainee at American States Insurance, and played in a semipro basketball league with a team from Anderson. Two years later Welmer moved back to Columbus, where he joined his father in the beer business.

In the fall of 1974, a fortuitous thing happened to Welmer. Jerry Newsom, an Indiana All-Star from Columbus in 1964, said to Welmer that since he liked basketball so much, he should get his referee license and they could work together. "I had no idea I'd wind up doing it full time," said Welmer.

Welmer had refereed in three Indiana high school state finals by age 34: Plymouth's double-overtime victory over Gary Roosevelt in the 1982 championship game, Warsaw's victory over New Castle in the afternoon in the 1984 tournament (Warsaw won state), and Marion's 1985 victory over Richmond in the championship game of its first of three successive state titles. That was the last high school game he worked.

In 1985-86 Welmer moved exclusively to college basketball, and continued to excel in a tough profession. How long will he keep chewing his plastic Fox 40 whistle (he'll go through around 20 whistles a season)?

"If my legs and general health stay reasonably good, I'd like to referee another three or four years and retire just before I reach 60," he said.

Chuck DeVoe

Park School, Indianapolis

Year graduated
1948

Major accomplishments
Nationally ranked as a junior tennis player; Received the Bunn
Trophy as Princeton's MVP in basketball as a senior; Was a member
of the group that formed the Indiana Pacers in 1967, and served as
president for seven years

For someone who never had the opportunity to showcase his athletic prowess against IHSAA teams because, at the time, Park School in Indianapolis was not a member of the organization, Chuck DeVoe has had a long and rewarding sporting life that is still active at age 76.

DeVoe is the oldest of three brothers who went on from Park, a college preparatory school, to play basketball and tennis at Princeton. John and Steve followed Chuck to the Ivy League school.

Colleges did not pound on DeVoe's door offering full-ride scholarships after he graduated from Park, which joined the IHSAA in 1979 under the name Park Tudor. "I think my tennis reputation was higher than in basketball, because I was ranked high in the country as a junior player," he said. "Whereas in basketball I'm sure nobody even knew I played."

DeVoe looked at Washington & Lee, William & Mary, and some other southern schools, because tennis was his big love at that time. A friend of the family convinced DeVoe's father and mother that he ought to take a look at Princeton, which does not offer athletic scholarships. He knew nothing about the school, but "on a lark" interviewed and was accepted.

"Fortunately my family was able to pay my way through," he said. "I boarded a train in Indianapolis, and got off at Princeton, never even having seen the campus prior. I only knew two or three people. I was a lost soul.

"I loved football in high school," continued DeVoe. "But I had to make a choice when I went to college, and I decided to concentrate on basketball and tennis. Obviously since I was in the backfield in high school I made a good choice, because otherwise Dick Kazmeier, one of my roommates at Princeton who won the Heisman Trophy in 1951, would have had me sitting on the bench all the time."

Although he played basketball at Park in anonymity, DeVoe feels he could have played with many IHSAA teams. "When I got into college, I got into some reasonably strong basketball and was able to play against some very good players," he said. "I felt like I held my own. I wasn't a superstar. I probably played as much as I did because I did what the coach, Cappy Cappon, told me to do. Our coach was a little like a Bobby Knight. He was very regimented. He played a very limited number of players. You either did it his way or you didn't do it. I think I played about 90 percent of the time as a junior and senior.

"As I look back, I thoroughly enjoyed all the sports I was involved in. I loved having my brothers follow me at Princeton. And, of course, John had a daughter, Ellen, who went later to Princeton and made a big name in basketball. An Indiana all-stater, she played center and may still hold some of the Princeton rebounding records. She probably did a better job than my brothers and I did."

At a Davis Cup match a few years ago at the Indianapolis Tennis Center, DeVoe was sitting at a table and heard a voice behind him say, "You played for Cappy Cappon." DeVoe turned and saw Knight, then at Indiana University. It was Knight's way of acknowledging that DeVoe was a fine college player.

"Knight knew my brother Steve," said DeVoe. "They went fishing together in Arkansas. We had a lot of interesting things to talk about because he coached at Army and Cappy Cappon was a well-known eastern coach."

DeVoe helped form the Indiana Pacers in 1967, serving as the team's president from December of 1968 to January of 1975. It was at this time that the original group of investors swallowed its losses and turned the team over to a group headed by the late Tom Binford.

"It was a big disappointment," said DeVoe, whose original investment was $30,000. "We put a lot of blood, sweat, and tears in that thing. Basically, we held it together with smoke and mirrors. I feel very strongly we did a helluva job in running that team, both with success on the floor [with ABA titles in 1970, '72, and '73], and minimizing our losses.

"A number of the heavy investors were close friends of mine that I had talked into it. They all agreed with me that we had a great run—we had a lot of fun, and we accomplished goal No. 1, which was to bring pro basketball to Indianapolis. With as much success as we had, I'm sure most of us would do it again."

DeVoe and Bill Bastian, who was on the original board, still share Pacer season tickets at Conseco Fieldhouse and they marvel at what they accomplished for Indianapolis.

"I think we got things started downtown," said DeVoe. "I think that everything that has happened since then was because we were able to get an arena, showcase a successful franchise, and show everyone what it did for the city, the kind of enthusiasm, and following you could build."

Tragically, John DeVoe died on December 14, 1968 while watching a Pacers game at the Indianapolis Coliseum. Chuck DeVoe, who succeeded John as the Pacers president, believes his brother might have become the Princeton coach had he taken a job as a Tiger assistant after visiting Cappon for a week. John declined the offer, returning to Indianapolis to enter the insurance business.

"John came home raving about a Princeton player by the name of Bill Bradley," said DeVoe. Soon thereafter, Cappon died of a heart attack in the Princeton locker room. DeVoe thinks John, who once scored 73 points in a game for Park and also won the Bunn Trophy as a Princeton senior, would have become the head coach if he had accepted Cappon's offer, because Princeton promoted from within.

After his military service, DeVoe joined the family business, the Leslie M. DeVoe company, a manufacturers representative firm in the electronics industry. DeVoe's son George now runs the company. DeVoe and his wife, Jody, have three adult children and seven grand-children.

DeVoe has accomplished very much in his remarkable journey through athletics. As a junior, he helped Princeton win the Michigan State holiday basketball tournament with victories over Ohio State and the Spartans. When he was a senior, he was named the MVP in the Michigan

State holiday basketball tournament, even though the Tigers lost to Minnesota and the Spartans in "pretty good games." While serving as a second lieutenant in the Army stationed in Korea, he helped build a basketball court and played games against other military teams serving in the area. In addition to that, DeVoe has played a tennis doubles match at the White House with Vice President George Bush as his partner against former Secretary of State Jim Baker. Bush and DeVoe won.

DeVoe says that as long as his body holds up, he will continue to circle the globe seeking to add to his impressive record in the Senior Cup amateur tennis competition, which he began competing in at age 55. By his 75th birthday, he had been on 17 U.S. Senior Cup teams that won eight world championships and took him to 16 different countries. In addition, he has won 21 national singles titles, 45 national doubles titles, and owned five European singles titles and seven doubles titles.

Ron Bonham

Muncie Central High School, Muncie

Year graduated
1960

Major accomplishments
Muncie Central's career scoring leader with 2,023 points; Scored 69
points in the 1960 state tournament final four; Mr. Basketball;
Indiana's MVP in two games against Kentucky in All-Star series;
Named as one of Indiana's finest 50 high school players in 1999;
Indiana Basketball Hall of Famer

The Blond Bomber isn't as blond as he once was when he played for
Muncie Central High School and the University of Cincinnati
Bearcats in the late 1950s and early '60s. Besides, now he only shoots
shotguns, not basketballs.

But Ron Bonham—Mr. Basketball of 1960 when he was a member of
Muncie Central's runner-up state tournament, 1962 NCAA champion with
Cincinnati, and NBA champion with the Boston Celtics in 1965 and '66—is
living a good life on the 52-acre property he and his wife, JJ, own in
Delaware County. Their property is a wildlife habitat that has quail, deer,
rabbits, ducks, and geese, and a six-acre wetland. Bonham, who doesn't feel
his 64 years, has been superintendent of the nearby Prairie Creek Reservoir
for the past 37 years.

"I had other opportunities while I was playing basketball that could have made me two or three times the money that I make out here [at Prairie Creek]," said Bonham, whose attractive wife is 10 years younger and has worked at the reservoir for 36 years. They have been married 33 years and have one daughter, Nicole.

"Even when I played with the Celtics, I don't know what my phone bill was, calling home almost every night. I'm just a homebody who likes to be with his bird dogs, sit and relax. I was always an outdoors person. That's the way my mother and father raised me, to respect our natural heritage. I probably belong to every conservation organization in the United States."

Ron doesn't hunt big game, but he does hunt duck and geese, and small game. "JJ is an outdoors person, too," he said. "We use the springer spaniels we raise. Madison gets to stay in the house. There are about 12 in the kennel. We've got a microwave out there for 'em and a couch. When you raise 'em from little guys up to 12 or 14 years old, they're like one of the family."

Bonham's journey to basketball stardom got off to a traumatic beginning when he was diagnosed with a heart murmur at a young age. He didn't participate in any sport, which was devastating to him, until he started to play basketball in the eighth grade. For 12 years, Ron tap danced and participated in acrobatics.

"That absolutely helped with my coordination and footwork, and also my vertical leap," he said. "I was one of those white guys that could jump. Back then you couldn't dunk [in a game]. But at 6-5 I could stand underneath the basket and slam dunk. I also had a turnaround jump shot that worked well for me."

Bonham was raised in a basketball atmosphere. His parents had season tickets at the Muncie Fieldhouse. Those tickets were "like hen's teeth to get," Ron said. "People even passed them down in their wills.

"My dad was a tremendous supporter. I had a basketball court behind my house, and I remember between the ninth grade and my sophomore year I cracked a bone in my left foot. I went through three walking casts working out. I never missed a day of shooting, even with the walking casts on. I wanted to be a Bearcat."

The late Bob Barnet, long-time sports editor of the Muncie Star, who is in the Indiana Basketball Hall of Fame, gave Bonham the nickname the Blond Bomber. He also called him the Muncie Rifle and the Muncie Mortar.

"I really miss Bob," said Bonham. "He was always a person I could call and we would talk. He would ask how the fishing was out here [at the reservoir]."

After Muncie Central lost to Crispus Attucks, eventual state champion, in the semistate of the 1959 tournament, the Bearcats dominated the '59-'60 season.

"Anytime you have five starters that go to Division I colleges, you've got talent," said Bonham, Muncie Central's career scoring leader with 2,023 points. "Jim Davis went to Colorado, John Dampier to Miami of Florida, Mike Jolley to DePaul, Jim Nettles to Wisconsin, and I went to Cincinnati.

"I averaged three-quarters of a game during the season, and the first two rounds of the tournament—we were beating teams that bad. Then we got to the state finals."

The Bearcats blew out Bloomington South, 102-66, with Bonham scoring 40 points. East Chicago Washington squeaked by Fort Wayne Central, 62-61. All the experts expected the Bearcats to easily complete a 32-0 record in the championship game, and claim Muncie Central's fifth state title. However, East Chicago stunned the Hoosier basketball world by defeating the Bearcats, 75-59, in what Bonham calls "the biggest disappointment in my basketball career."

He says, "East Chicago had a tremendous team. We were ranked No. 1 and they were ranked No. 2, No. 3 throughout most of the season. The people that saw them knew they had talent, but it was just one of those game where I personally didn't get the rest between games that I should have. We thought we were going to win. I had 21 points in the first half, but I burned out."

Bonham fouled out with about nine minutes left, the only time he fouled out in high school. He ended up with 29 points for a record of 69 for the two games in the finals, but his patented turnaround jump shot misfired when it counted.

"I watch that film over and over again, and I don't how many shots made it to the rim and didn't go over it. Everything I shot that second half was short."

Bonham bombed away in the 1960 All-Star games, scoring 32 points in a 95-86 loss to Kentucky in Indianapolis, and 27 in a 101-64 victory in Louisville. He was named MVP in both games. His 59 total points rank him third among Indiana players all-time in the series, behind George McGinnis (76) and Oscar Robertson (75).

Purdue wooed Bonham heavily, and he even enrolled at the West Lafayette school, but he didn't attend any classes. Instead he accepted an invitation from friend Larry Elsasser who wanted him to go to the University of Cincinnati.

"Larry loved to hunt and fish, and we hit it off so well that we roomed together all four years in college. I wanted to stay in Indiana, but I was really torn. I had watched Oscar Robertson at Cincinnati. Purdue was a football school. Basketball was second. Basketball was No. 1 at Cincinnati, football was second. No one could have had a better time in college than we had, and nothing but success."

Cincinnati won two national titles, and was a runner-up while Bonham was a Bearcat. He wasn't eligible for the varsity his freshman season when the Bearcats beat Ohio State, 70-65, in overtime in the 1961 title game.

"When I was a sophomore, we beat Ohio State, Jerry Lucas, John Havlicek and that group, 71-59, in the championship game."

Cincinnati went for a third successive title in 1963, when Bonham was a junior. "We should have won that year, too," he said. "We had Loyola of Chicago down, but they beat us in overtime." Cincinnati led 45-30, but Loyola managed to tie the score at 54-54 on Jerry Harkness' basket that sent the game into overtime. Loyola won, 60-58.

Harkness and Bonham became teammates on the Indiana Pacers' first team in 1967-68. "We talked many times about that game," said Bonham, whose Cincinnati coach, Ed Jucker, called him one of the greatest pure shooters he had ever seen. "We had practiced probably two weeks on their zone press—that's what they were known for. I didn't touch the ball for the last eight minutes of the game. I had 20 or 21 points. Usually we started stalling the last eight minutes or so, but we started with 12 minutes to go. The fellow guarding me turned and congratulated me and said, 'Great game.' He had already given up. But the momentum changed."

Bonham received a ring when Cincinnati won the 1962 NCAA championship, and a gold watch and a diamond ring when the Celtics won NBA titles in 1965 and '66. What he got with the Pacers was the mumps. He missed almost two months of the season.

"Everything was first class with the Celtics," he said. "That first year of the ABA everything wasn't organized. With the Pacers, we'd sit in airports all night. I really missed being at home."

The Chicago Bulls picked Bonham from the Pacers in an expansion draft, but he retired to his favorite county. He served 12 years as a Delaware County commissioner while handling duties at the reservoir. Ron has lost most of the sight in his left eye because of melanoma. "That did away with my depth perception," he said. "I can't shoot a basketball anymore. It didn't affect my shooting with a shotgun, because I always close my left eye anyway."

In 1991 Bonham was inducted into the Indiana Basketball Hall of Fame and in 1999 he was named one of Indiana's finest 50 players of all-time. He has it in his will that all the rings, watches, and trophies he's received in his illustrious career will go to either the state or Delaware County hall of fame.

"I don't know how many memorabilia businesses have contacted me whether I would want to sell those," said Ron. "There's no way I could ever sell something like that."

Darnell Archey

New Castle High School, New Castle

Year graduated
1999

Major accomplishments
Ranked seventh all-time career scorer at New Castle High with 1,103
points; Set Butler's career free-throw percentage record at .953;
Ranked second on Butler's all-time career three-point field goal list with
217; Holds the NCAA Division I record for 85 consecutive free throws;
Won the NCAA three-point shootout during 2003 Final Four

New Castle not only has the largest high school gym in the United
States, but it also has the Indiana Basketball Hall of Fame, which is
one of the finest facilities of its kind in the world and produces
some of the straightest shooters in the sport.

When Darnell Archey saw his Butler University career three-point
record of 217 broken by Bruce Horan in a victory over Tulane on November
30, 2005, the former Bulldog shooting guard broke into a huge smile.

"I have to take my hat off to Bruce for two reasons," said Archey, who
set the NCAA Division I record for 85 consecutive free throws before going
on to win the national three-point shootout during the 2003 NCAA Final
Four at New Orleans. "One, because we're the best of friends, and two,
because he's a New Castle guy like me. The New Castle guys have to stick
together. Everybody always picks on us because we come from such a small
town. The joke is we're such good shooters because we have nothing else to
do in New Castle."

New Castle has one of the best high school basketball traditions in Indiana. The Trojans won the town's only state championship in 1932, in addition to having had 10 Indiana All-Stars and two Mr. Basketballs: Kent Benson in 1973 and Steve Alford in 1983, both of whom helped Indiana University win NCAA championships in 1976 and 1987, respectively.

Locals will never forget the famous "Church Street Shootout" when Kokomo's Jimmy Rayl, who became Mr. Basketball in the 1958-59 season, had 49 points in the last regular-season game in the tiny Church Street gym. This gym later became the YMCA where Archey played as a youngster. New Castle's Ray Pavy, who was the No. 2 Indiana All-Star that season, outscored Rayl by two points in New Castle's 92-81 victory on February 20, 1959. Combined, they scored 100 points. Another memorable New Castle moment came on March 19, 1983, when Alford scored 57 points in a 79-64 semistate victory over Indianapolis Broad Ripple in Hinkle Fieldhouse. It is the highest total ever recorded in the state tournament.

Archey played junior varsity basketball as a high school freshman before being moved up to varsity. There he scored 1,103 points in three years, becoming seventh on the all-time career list. In the 1996-97 season, the last of one-class basketball in Indiana, New Castle was 19-1 in the regular season. The Trojans met Batesville in the regional championship game.

"That was the first time I ever played before a sold-out crowd in the fieldhouse," said Archey. "They were turning people away. We wound up winning in overtime, 61-58. They were comparing them to Milan. We thought after that game we might get to the final four. At the semistate in Hinkle Fieldhouse we played Franklin and they upset us, 76-65."

The Trojans finished 24-2 in 1997. In Archey's junior season, New Castle went 15-6, losing to No. 1 Anderson in the sectional. The next year, the Trojans, 16-8, won the sectional, but lost to Indianapolis North Central and Jason Gardner in the regional at Anderson, 62-58. North Central won the state championship that season.

As a junior, Archey committed to Butler. "When I walked onto that campus, I fell in love with the place," he said. "My only concern was that previous season I went one for nine from the three-point line against Franklin in the semistate. I wasn't sure I could shoot there. But I remember right before I met with coach Barry Collier, my dad and I went out to the Hinkle Fieldhouse. I think I missed only two shots in a five-minute span. I then knew I could shoot there."

In his four years at Butler, Archey played for three different coaches, Collier for one year, Thad Matta for one year, and Lickliter for two years.

"It wasn't easy," said Archey. "The only thing that changed, basically, was the coach. We had the same kids, the same style of play, the same defense."

The Bulldogs didn't miss a beat in those four years. They were 23-8 in 1999-2000, and lost to Florida, 69-68, in overtime in the NCAA tournament on a last-second shot by Mike Miller. The next season Butler went 24-8 and beat No. 23 Wake Forest, 79-63, in the NCAA tournament before losing to No. 4 Arizona, 73-52. In Archey's junior season, the Bulldogs were 26-6, and lost in the NIT tournament at Syracuse, 66-65, in overtime. The Bulldogs were 100-28 in those four seasons with "New Castle guys" playing major roles.

In the 2002-2003 season, New Castlers Brandon Miller and Archey, seniors, and Horan, freshman, played for Coach Todd Lickliter at Butler. In addition to setting a school record of 27 wins, they were the first Bulldog team to make it to the Sweet Sixteen of the NCAA tournament. In the first rounds, they defeated No. 20 Mississippi, 47-46, on a last-second shot by Miller; and No. 14 Louisville, 79-71, with Archey sinking eight of nine three-point shots. However, Butler's dream season ended in the first game of the Sweet Sixteen at Albany, N.Y. when the Bulldogs lost to No. 3 Oklahoma, 65-54.

Archey played four seasons at Butler. He finished with 985 career points, a .443 three-point percentage, and a school record of a .953 free-throw percentage. Miller, who received the 2003 Chip Hilton Player of the Year Award—presented to an NCAA Division I men's player for outstanding character, leadership, integrity, humility, sportsmanship and talent—is 23rd in Butler's all-time scoring with 1,121 points. He is third on the three-point career list with 189 in three seasons. He went to Southwest Missouri State as a freshman to play for Alford, and when Steve went to Iowa, Brandon transferred to Butler. Bruce Horan finished his Butler career with 314 three-point baskets, second most in Horizon League history behind Rashad Phillips of Detroit, who had 348. Horan had 113 three-pointers in his senior season, and finished with a streak of 80 games with a three-pointer, second-longest in NCAA history to the 88 held by Illinois' Cory Bradford from 1998-2001. Darrin Fitzgerald of Butler holds the NCAA record of 158 three-pointers in one season set in 1986-87.

Archey says it was a goal of Miller, Joel Cornette, and himself "to put Butler on the map. We always talked about what Gonzaga did. That's what we wanted to do, get us in the national spotlight. Then we got to the Sweet Sixteen and all the focus was on us. It was awesome. We didn't really have a go-to guy. There was a different leading scorer almost every night. Everybody said we played basketball how it's meant to be played, sharing the ball, playing tough defense and every guy, one through 12, having that 'never-quit' attitude. A lot of times we were the smallest team out there. But our hearts were huge."

Dennis Archey always insisted that his son should "shoot to swish," because thinking that way would always give him more arch if he was in a slump. He also insisted upon having a routine when shooting free throws. Archey would straddle the nail holes by the foul line to make sure that he was perfectly in line with the basket, bend his knees, and dribble three times. He said, "That was my magic number."

Archey has a lot of magic numbers: he made free throws in 11 different arenas in 57 games against 22 different opponents (31 at home, 33 on the road, and 21 at neutral sites), he didn't miss a free throw in the entire 2001-2002 season (23 of 23); and, the most free throws he made in any game was eight at Indiana State on December 5, 2002.

"During my sophomore season I remember Gary Buchanan from Villanova set the record for successive free throws at 73," said Darnell. "I set my goal to get 74 in a row, but I never thought I'd get there. I didn't get fouled a whole lot. In my junior year I only shot 23. Probably half of them were off technical fouls.

"A funny thing was it didn't matter if I was on the bench or in a game, Coach Lickliter always had me shoot free throws off technical fouls on the other team. The first time that happened was against IU in the championship game of the Hoosier Classic at Conseco Fieldhouse in 2002. Late in the second half, IU coach Mike Davis got a technical foul. Coach Lickliter sent me in. I had thought it was illegal for a guy to come off the bench and shoot technical foul free throws, so I had a big grin on my face shooting them."

It was during a tournament in Hawaii that Archey sank nine free throws to tie Buchanan's record. He broke the record with his first free throw in the next game on January 4, 2003, at the University of Illinois-Chicago, a game Butler won, 68-65. The streak ended four games later in a 64-60 home victory over Youngstown State when Archey missed his first of two free throws. "The pressure was really getting to me," he said. "Steve Alford called me after I finally missed. He told me he would shoot free throws in his backyard. I think his record was 216 in a row. Steve said that now, as he neared that, his body would just shut down. That's how I felt. I thought it was pretty special that Steve and his father, Sam, called me."

Archey credits Brad Stevens, Butler assistant coach, with a major assist in getting him paired against Matt Bonner, Florida; Kent Williams, Southern Illinois; Kyle Korver, Creighton; Tom Coverdale, Indiana; Willie Deane, Purdue; Jason Gardner, Arizona; and Hollis Price, Oklahoma in the 2003 Men's Collegiate Three-Point Championship.

"They wanted bigger school names, but Brad kept calling about me," said Archey. "When we made the Sweet Sixteen that helped my case. I thought I could win, but I remember shooting my first three and my legs locked up. Luckily I made the final four contestants and after that I had my confidence."

Korver was favored to win the shootout, but Archey beat him and Bonner out to claim the men's title. "I was a jump shooter and eventually that bit me, because I was tired," he said. "I went against Amy Wahl, the women's winner from Fort Wayne. She beat me. I lost to a girl, they always say, but it was nice her being from Indiana."

Archey's plan to play professionally in Australia didn't work out, so he used his marketing degree to get into business. A few months later he decided that if he couldn't play basketball any more he would coach. He was assistant varsity coach at Carmel High School in 2004-2005 and then took over as Carmel junior varsity coach the next season.

Of his Butler career, Archey says, "I thought I overachieved. I had aspirations of going to the NCAA tournament and hitting big-time shots, but I wasn't very big, so I thought it would never happen. Now I want to be a high school basketball coach because I want to be a state champion in Indiana."

If he made it happen as a New Castle guy at Butler, who's to say he can't make it happen as an Indiana high school coach?

Cam Cameron

Terre Haute South, Terre Haute

Year graduated
1979

Major accomplishments
Competed in three consecutive state tournament finals;
Received the Trester Award for mental attitude at the 1979 finals;
Indiana All-Star

Hubie Brown might not remember the incident, but Cam Cameron certainly does. It occurred at a basketball camp in Cameron Indoor Stadium at Duke University when Cameron was in the first grade.

"I guess I wasn't paying attention like I should've, nodding off in the front row, and the next thing you know a leather basketball hit me right in the head and knocked me over," said Cameron, former Indiana University quarterback and ex-head football coach of the Hoosiers. Brown, NBA television analyst who then was on Duke's coaching staff headed by Bucky Waters, threw the ball.

"He got my attention," said Cameron, now offensive coordinator of the San Diego Chargers. "He said, 'Cameron, listen up when I'm talking.' That memory just kind of flashes back in my mind. I do a pretty good job, and have over the years, of staying awake even in the most boring meetings."

Cameron was introduced to football in the third grade at Durham, and had success early. He helped his team, which played games in the outfield of the Durham Bulls' baseball stadium; win a state title with a 13-0 record.

In the third grade, Cam's parents divorced. Four years later he, his older sister Betsy, mother Barbara, and her boyfriend, Tom Harp, moved to Terre Haute, Indiana, where Harp became football coach at Indiana State University. Barbara and Tom were married a year later when Cameron was a student at Honey Creek Junior High School.

It didn't take Cameron long to become an adopted Hoosier. "When you're raised by a single mom, life can be a little hectic," he said. "I didn't know what I was getting into when I moved to Indiana. One thing everybody would say, 'It's a basketball state.' Boy, it didn't take me long to figure out what they were talking about."

Cameron went on to help Terre Haute South advance to the state high school basketball tournament finals three straight years, 1977 through 1979; win the Trester Award as a senior; earn a spot on the 1979 Indiana All-Star team; be offered a football scholarship at Indiana University; and became a member of Bob Knight's basketball team for three years as a walk-on.

During Cam's summers in Terre Haute he lived an Indiana boy's dream. Early in the morning, he would either ride his bike or ride with his stepfather to the ISU arena. He would lift weights, shoot baskets, and throw a football.

"At about two o'clock, Larry Bird would come in from his summer job and start shooting around," said Cameron. "I was kinda waiting for Larry to get in. I would have the opportunity to play H-O-R-S-E with him almost every day, which was really a treat. Then at about 3:30, all the Indiana State players would come from their summer jobs and meet at the arena. Usually Larry or one of the coaches would pick the teams. They always needed a 10th guy, so they let me play. We played from four to six Monday through Thursday. That's where I developed as a player."

Although he is one of the few Indiana basketball players ever to make it to the state finals three years in a row, Cameron never won a championship. South lost to East Chicago Washington, 66-45, in the first game of the 1977 tournament; to Muncie Central, 65-64, in overtime in the title game of the 1978; and to Muncie Central again, 60-55, in overtime in the second game of the 1979 tournament.

Of those three successive appearances in Market Square Arena at Indianapolis, Cameron said, "As I look at the success I was able to have personally, it was directly related to the kind of teammates I had. Richard Wilson and I were on all three of those teams. He's not a guy who gets talked about a lot. He probably was one of the most talented guys to come out of Terre Haute. He started as a sophomore, and I came off the bench as the sixth man. We only had one senior on that '77 team, a guy named Mike Joyner, who led our team. He was killed a year later in the Evansville plane crash."

Cameron recalls 1978 as a memorable year. "We played Washington and Steve Bouchie, who was Mr. Basketball in 1979, in the semistate at Evansville. It was probably the greatest game I've ever been associated with. They were 25-0, and No. 1 in state. We were down like 12 points with two or three minutes to go, and came back to win."

In that year's title game, Wilson had the fans on their feet. His field goal from the 10-second line sent the game into overtime, tied 62-62. He connected again from far out in the last two seconds of overtime, making the score 65-64. South called time out with one second left. The Bearcats threw the ball away, and South's Tony Watson took a shot from midcourt with one second left that missed.

"You know what beat us [in the title game]?" said Cameron. "Merrillville beat the tar out of us in the first game. Wilson and Kevin Thompson both had to go to the hospital between games. A lot of people don't know that. Kevin hurt his back and Richard had a rib injury. I think we played a courageous game at night, but we didn't play as well as we could. And Jackie Moore just ran circles around us [scoring 27 points for his team]."

After South lost to the Bearcats again in the '79 state finals, Cameron thought the family might head home to Terre Haute before the title game the Bearcats won, 64-60, over Anderson, because the players were exhausted. Instead, he wound up accepting the Trester Award.

"That's the only award you would see if you came to my house [in Coronado, California]," Cameron said with obvious pride.

After graduation from South, Cameron received an appointment to the Naval Academy to play football and basketball. He was also recruited by Nebraska and Michigan State for basketball, but opted to accept coach Lee Corso's offer of a football scholarship to Indiana University.

The lure of playing basketball in Assembly Hall didn't diminish, however, and after Cam's sophomore football season he went to Corso and said he would like to see if Knight would let him try out for basketball.

"You want to be a coach, and what better person would there be to learn from," were Corso's encouraging words.

It took three trips to Knight's office before the coach looked Cameron in the eye and said, "It's just not gonna work. I've never brought a guy from the outside on the team during the season."

Cameron told Knight he would be ready if the coach needed him. Knight told Cameron that if something did happen, "We'll call you."

Something did happen some 10 days later. One of the players, Rick Rowray, broke his arm in practice on a Sunday. Cameron waited anxiously for his phone to ring on Monday, and finally it did. Assistant coach Jim Crews invited Cameron to come out for the team. Cameron was at practice at 2:30 p.m., and even got to play about 12 minutes at Kentucky the following Thursday.

"We got killed, and that's why I got to play," laughed Cam. In his first two years with Knight, Cameron played in 30 games and scored 33 points, all significant totals to the native Tar Heel.

After Cameron's junior season in football, Corso got fired and Sam Wyche replaced him. "It's funny," said Cam. "People mention I'm a football guy. Going into my fifth year, Coach Knight was going to put me on basketball scholarship, and I was not going to play football. When Wyche got hired, Coach Knight said, 'You might be able to learn something from this guy.' Taking Knight's advice was one of the best moves I ever made. Unfortunately I got hurt in the next-to-last game of the season."

Because he had to wear a knee brace, Cameron could not play basketball his final season at IU, but he remained with the team. He treasures that season because he met Knight's stipulation that fifth-year players had to have completed their undergraduate courses, and be working on their Master's, and because Knight steered him to a doctor the coach said was the best in the world for knee surgery.

"Knight also said, 'Just because you're hurt, the expectations on you are no different,'" stated Cameron. " 'You're to be at every meeting, every practice, you'll make the trips, and we expect you, as a senior, to help lead this basketball team.' It was a great feeling to still be able to contribute. Steve Alford was a freshman that year, and we beat North Carolina in the NCAA Mideast Regional at Atlanta when they had Michael Jordan.

"I had a phenomenal experience with Coach Knight. What he did for me in my personal life, the discipline to my life, and the things he taught me were just tremendous. It's nice to still have that friendship to this day."

Cameron is trying to instill the positive things he learned from all of his coaches in Hoosierland—Don McDonald, basketball at Honey Creek Junior High; Gordon Neff, South basketball; Bob Clements, South football; Corso, Wyche and Knight—and in the four children that he and his wife, Missy, have: Tommy, 12; Danny, 10; Christopher, eight; and Elizabeth, five.

"I consider it a privilege to have been a part of Indiana high school basketball," he said. "It's unique. Everywhere I go people talk about the movie Hoosiers. I did live that movie other than we didn't win the state championship like Milan did."

Dave Colescott

Terre Haute South, Terre Haute

Year graduated
1979

Major accomplishments
State champion in 1975 and 1976; Leading scorer in the final four
games of the 1976 tournament with 96 points; The second player in
history to win a state title, receive the Trester Award for mental
attitude, and become Mr. Basketball in the same year (1976);
Starter at North Carolina as a junior and senior; Indiana Basketball
Hall of Famer

Bats swirled around Dave Colescott and two of his sisters, Linda
and Susie, as they sat in Hinkle Fieldhouse on March 22, 1969,
watching their father Jack's Marion Giants basketball team play an
important game against Indianapolis Washington. For the second year in a
row, Jack Colescott's team lost a squeaker in the afternoon round of the state
high school tournament finals, 61-60. Marion had lost the year before in the
same setting, falling to Indianapolis Shortridge, 58-56. Dave Colescott
remembers that a third sister, Nancy, was on the floor as a cheerleader and
that his mother, Marge, was sitting right behind her husband, where "she
needed to be." Colescott recalls that it was hard to watch the game, because
it was so close and the clock didn't work.

"After the game I was disgusted," he said. "I was just 12 years old and I
wanted to be with my father, and I couldn't get to him. I made a pledge that
when I got [to the state finals], we were going to make sure we did it for him.

We felt really bad for my dad, because he put his heart and soul into the players, and he ran a first-class team. The team went to church together—they were perfect role models—things you don't see as much as you'd like to. They were my heroes."

Jack Colescott, who is in the Indiana Basketball Hall of Fame, was quick to say, "You don't think Dave is prejudiced, do you?"

Colescott interjected, "My dad is very humble. I'm not as humble as he is. I guess unassuming would be the right word, but he basically built the program in the early '60s and up until what it became, one of the great powerhouses of Indiana high school basketball."

Colescott, who also was a state champion in 1975, didn't get to play for his father, because Jack retired as Marion coach in 1971. He wanted his son to have as normal a high school basketball career as possible without worrying about the pressure of playing for his father. In the meantime, the Marion athletic director's job became available and Jack took it.

"Dave didn't have to worry about his dad showing any favoritism," Jack said. He was involved in hiring the new coach, and ironically, he chose Bill Green—the man who had coached Washington to an unbeaten season and state championship in 1969.

Jack and Bill were Indiana Central alums (the school is now named the University of Indianapolis), and knew each other well. "I thought we made a good choice, and Dave was fortunate to play for a guy that would bring out the best in him," said Jack, who is retired and living with his wife in Gas City, Indiana.

Colescott laughed when he heard his father's comment about the man who wound up winning five state titles at Marion: '75, '76, '87, '88 and '89, giving him six overall, the most by any coach in history.

"For the first two years I played in high school I didn't forgive [Green] for what happened to Marion in 1969," he said. "I quickly learned to love and respect him very much." Colescott says all he remembered about Green at the '69 tournament "was his loud sweater. I thought he was a hippie or something." In 1969, Green wore purple sweaters, Washington's color. At Marion he wore yellow sweaters, Marion's color.

"And talk about changing your life," said Colescott. "He got me into country music. Every day he'd come in and listen to that stuff. We were into rock 'n roll. He would say, 'The rednecks are going to rule the world someday.' He loved basketball, fishing, hunting, listening to country music, and loud sweaters."

During the 1976 state finals, in which unranked Marion beat Jeffersonville, 49-47, and Rushville, 82-76, the Giants played a song by Waylon Jennings, "Luckenbach, Texas," in the dressing room for good luck. They finished 23-5. In 1975, the Giants wound up 28-1 after defeating Lebanon, 73-65, and Loogootee, 58-46, in the state finals.

After the '75 championship game, Green said, "I was particularly happy for the Colescott family, because Jack took a couple of outstanding teams to the state and lost both times in the closing seconds. Jack probably should have had a gold ring, and now he has the satisfaction of watching his son Colescott win a state championship ring."

By the time the Giants reached the outskirts of Marion after that '75 victory, it was past midnight, but an estimated 10,000 people lined the road into town. The players rode around the town square on fire trucks, then headed to their gym, where it was so crowded they had to stand on folding chairs.

"I've never seen such pandemonium," said Colescott. "Even my grandfather, who was around 85 and never got to go to the games because of his health, was in the crowd."

The following year Jack decided to have Green keep the team in Indianapolis after the championship game so the fans could get home at a decent hour and be fresh for a celebration the next afternoon in the gym. Jack says the emotional reaction of the fans those two years is what Hoosier Hysteria is all about. "It's hard to put into words, but Hoosier Hysteria, wherever the name came from, aptly describes Indiana basketball, high school level."

Colescott was the second-leading scorer in the final four games of the 1975 state tournament with 68 points (teammate Kevin Pearson was high with 72), and he was the leading scorer in the final four games of the 1976 state tournament with 96 points. Colescott helped Indiana win two games over Kentucky in the All-Star series.

Receiving the Trester Award was an overwhelming experience, says Colescott. "It was almost too much. Why me? My cup is full, winning state two years in a row, then to have that on top of it, which I think was a tremendous honor to be told you're the winner of the mental attitude award, because that was emphasized to me as a young guy. That's probably why I never got a technical or thrown out of games. I was not afraid of my father, but it was very clear that you had to do it the right way. I was always told to keep my mouth shut and play."

Jack Colescott knew Purdue recruiter Bob King, and Colescott thought he probably would go there. But the Boilermakers, he said, had four "pretty good guards: Jerry Sichting, Kyle Macy, Eugene Parker and Bruce Parkinson. I thought I was good, but my gosh, I wasn't any better than those four. I'd love to have played there, but we opted for other places."

Jack treasures the letter he got from Bob King saying it would be unfair to recruit Colescott with all of the talent ahead of him at Purdue. Michigan, Illinois, and Notre Dame were in the picture for basketball, and Clemson for baseball (Colescott was a shortstop), but he chose to go to North Carolina and play for coach Dean Smith.

"I really liked the people in Chapel Hill and the tradition," said Colescott. "In high school we won most of the time, and I liked to win and be a part of a great program." How was his career as a Tar Heel? They were 95-27 in Colescott's four years, losing to Marquette, 67-59, in the 1977 NCAA championship game. He averaged 4.9 points in 103 games as a Tar Heel.

"I had a storybook career at Marion," said Colescott, "and I felt it was going to be like that at UNC. Well, there's nothing better than humbling yourself, whether it's not playing a lot your first year. I had an All-ACC point guard, Phil Ford, to compete against every day, and I broke my foot the first year.

"Then a tragic thing my sophomore year, that looking back, I think affected me more was my grandfather passed away. It took me a few months to get my head straight, because he definitely was one of my mentors. But I bounced back and started my junior and senior years [and was co-captain as a senior]. I think my role changed from being the one go-to player as a high school senior, to more like it was my junior year at Marion. We were all pretty solid players. I liked playing like that."

Colescott was drafted by Utah in the seventh round of the NBA draft, and had two tryouts with the Jazz. He was cut the first time, and then broke his ankle playing one-on-one against Matt Doherty, former UNC player and coach. "I always thought I'd be like John Havlicek or Larry Bird waving to the crowd when you're done playing after a great career. My career ended in a sweaty gymnasium in a pickup game."

Colescott and his wife, April, who have three children, the youngest of which is named after his grandfather, live in Winston-Salem, North Carolina, where Colescott is vice-president of sales for Hanes Hosiery. Young Jack, eight, appears to be the one to carry on the Colescott athletic legacy.

"My dad used to tell me sports is just like life, one day you're going to be on top of the mountain, the next day you can be in the valley," said Colescott. "I've had a lot of good things happen and a lot of things that seemed like bad things at the time. But I think it makes you better a person."

Louie Dampier

Southport High School, Indianapolis

Year graduated
1963

Major accomplishments
Set sectional records for points in a game (40), and total points (114);
Indiana All-Star; All-American in 1967 at the University of Kentucky;
Academic All-American as a junior and senior; Indiana Basketball Hall
of Famer

For someone who shot two-handed over his head through his freshman year at Southport High School in Indianapolis, Louie Dampier has had a wonderful basketball career. During the 2005-2006 season, Dampier, who is 61 and living in retirement in LaGrange, Kentucky, was still playing in a 50-and-over league on Sunday afternoons in the old Jeffersonville, Indiana, high school gym where he played as a senior at Southport.

"I love the game," said Dampier, who played for the legendary University of Kentucky coach, Adolph Rupp. "I feel fortunate I still can run up and down. I've never had a knee problem or really ever sprained an ankle."

How long does the man who holds eight all-time ABA records and is a member of the Indiana Basketball Hall of Fame, plan to keep playing?

"I'm starting to think about it," he said. "My wife, Judy, doesn't listen if I come home with an ache or a pain. I still enjoy playing in pickup games Tuesday and Thursday nights over in Indiana at a little gym called Colgate."

The other veterans never get to see Dampier's two-handed shot over the head. "No, they get to see the long last-second shot," he said with a laugh. And they don't play with a red, white, and blue ball, the staple of the ABA.

"I'm mostly into assists now," Dampier added. "I don't want to work hard enough to get open. I didn't like the red, white, and blue ball at first. The early ones were slick. But they started changing the way they made them, and after that I preferred the red, white, and blue ball."

The youngest of five kids—three girls and two boys—Dampier watched his brothers-in-law play at Southport when he was young. "They would come over to the house, so that's how I got to shooting two-handed over my head." During the winter, Dampier would pound snow into tight mounds so that he could get closer to the rim on the basket his dad had built.

Dampier says he was fairly accurate with the two-handed shot, but that he didn't think it would get him very far. When he began his sophomore season at Southport, his freshman coach asked him where he learned the jump shot he was shooting. Dampier said, "I don't know. It wasn't at a camp or anything. I just did it on my own."

As a sophomore, Dampier played mostly jayvee ball, then would dress with the varsity and sit most of the time. When a varsity player got hurt in a sectional game, coach Blackie Braden told him to go in.

"We lost the game, our last of the season, but I hit like four shots," he said. "I only remember taking the first shot, I was so nervous. After the game Coach Braden said something about next year, 'Right Louie?' I said, 'Okay,' and I thought to myself, 'I guess I'll get to play varsity next year.'"

The Cardinals lost in the regional final of the state tournament in Dampier's two varsity seasons, but in the sectional tournament during his senior year, Dampier set records for points in a game (40) and total points (114). Braden used to kiddingly say that Rupp just happened to be passing through Indianapolis one wintry night that season when he decided to watch Dampier play. It wasn't a chance happening, according to Dampier.

"Coach Rupp had a recruiter, and he came up and wanted to talk to guys like Bill Russell of Columbus and some of the other big names," Dampier said. "When he was in Columbus, he said, 'Is there anybody around here you think I can look at?' They said, 'Yeah, Louie Dampier at Southport.' He came up to one of our practices and sat next to my brother, and was asking a lot of questions about me. My brother wouldn't tell him, because he thought he might be a scout for another team. He finally got to talk to me and watched practice, and he may have come to a game. He went back and told Adolph to recruit me."

Rupp had never heard of Dampier. He usually took the word of his recruiter on a prospect, but he wanted to see Dampier play, so he journeyed to Indianapolis for a reason.

"It was a game I think against Broad Ripple and the first half I was like 9-for-11," said Dampier. "Coach Rupp left at halftime, and that's how I ended up at Kentucky."

Growing up in Indiana, Dampier wanted to go to Indiana University. An uncle took him to visit coach Branch McCracken, who met with the uncle and not Dampier. After the meeting, McCracken told Dampier, "You have a scholarship if you want it." Dampier felt that his uncle had talked McCracken into offering a scholarship, and he decided then to go visit Kentucky.

"Some people at Indiana University were upset with me that I didn't go to Indiana, and even my family," said Dampier.

Braden prepared Dampier well for his career in Lexington, Kentucky, playing for the coach known as The Baron. "Coach Braden had discipline and he was tough on the players. That's the one thing I took with me when I went to play for Coach Rupp. He was very strict and he had his rules, and you had to abide by them. That ran some players off. They played a year or two and couldn't take it any longer. I was kinda used to it from Blackie Braden."

The Wildcat players couldn't talk in practice, says Dampier. "You could ask a question or holler out there was a pick coming, but just talk among us, we couldn't do it." One day when the team was going over Tennessee scouting reports, Dampier tried to tell Rupp he couldn't get through a pick, and the players needed to switch. All Dampier got out was the word "but." Rupp barked at Dampier, who thought, "Boy, this is it." "But after practice I went to talk to him and everything was fine."

Like Bob Knight, now coaching at Texas Tech after winning three NCAA titles at Indiana University, Rupp was a tough taskmaster, but there was a significant difference.

"Rupp's assistant coach, Harry Lancaster, was kind of the enforcer. Anything physical was him. Coach Rupp was verbal. The difference between

Coach Rupp and Coach Knight is that Coach Rupp could be in the huddle just giving you whatever, but not one fan would know it, where Coach Knight would not try to hide anything. Everybody in the gymnasium knew he was chewing out one of his players."

The Wildcats made the NCAA tournament in Dampier's junior year, when they advanced to the Final Four in 1966 at Cole Fieldhouse on the University of Maryland campus. Kentucky was ranked No. 1, Duke No. 2, and Texas Western November 3. Utah, unranked, was the other entrant.

Kentucky, dubbed affectionately "Rupp's Runts" by the Wildcat fans because no starter was taller than 6-foot-5, defeated Duke, 83-79, and Texas Western (now Texas El Paso) beat Utah, 85-78. That set up one of the most historic NCAA championship matchups in history. Kentucky was all white, and Texas Western's top eight players were black.

The Miners ended Rupp's quest for a fifth NCAA title, 72-65. It was a "heartbreaking" loss, says Dampier, who added that Texas Western was "a good team." What is more disconcerting to Dampier is that there was a lot of talk about Rupp being a racist.

"Rupp wasn't racist," Dampier said emphatically. "I don't understand it myself. It's just that Texas Western started all black players and we were an all-white team. It was historic in that a black team beat a white team to win the NCAA championship, but Coach Rupp never once made a statement or anything about race going into the game.

"I've had a lot of people call me on the anniversary of the game and interview me, and they never put what I say in the paper, because it isn't what they want to hear. I got so confused I started asking the players that were on my team, 'Did I miss something? Was there something said before the game, during, halftime, or anything about the racial factor involved?,' and they said no."

Dampier believes it was merely a game between two good college teams. "We had already beaten a Michigan team in the region final that I think started three or four black players. It wasn't the first time we played against black players. To me it was the championship game and just another team.

Dampier's decision to leave Indiana for Kentucky "turned out just great," he says. He was all-Southeastern Conference three times, and All-America in 1967. As a junior and senior he was Academic All-America.

Cincinnati of the NBA drafted Dampier, but he would have had to try out for the team, so he opted to sign with the Colonels, who offered the 6-foot guard a contract. He played nine seasons with Kentucky, winning one title in 1975 by beating the Indiana Pacers, 4-1. When the ABA and NBA merged in 1976, Dampier had all-time red, white, and blue records for games played (728), minutes played (27,770), points (13,726), field goals made (5,290), field goals attempted (12,047), three-pointers made (794), three-pointers attempted (2,217), and assists (4,044)

Before the 1976-77 season began, Dampier called Bob Leonard, coach of the Indiana Pacers, but "he needed a big guy, so he wasn't going to take me in the dispersal draft. I would have loved to go to Indiana. Fortunately, San Antonio drafted me, another ABA team." He played three years with the Spurs. Dampier went to the New York Nets camp in 1979, but was cut on the final day of training camp.

"I had a nice career," he said in a major understatement. After working for a time in sales, Dampier started his own audio and videotape company, Dampier Distributing. He sold it in 1998 when he took an assistant coaching job with the Denver Nuggets.

"The four years I had with the Nuggets was enough for me," said Dampier. "There's a lot of stress and pressure. The only thing I miss about it is the players. They're great."

Lee Hamilton

Evansville Central High School, Evansville

Year graduated
1948

Major accomplishments
Received Trester Award for mental attitude; Served in the U.S. House
of Representatives for 34 years, from 1965 to 1999; Named a Living
Legend by the Indiana Historical Society for his distinguished
Congressional service; Indiana Basketball Hall of Famer

Nancy Hamilton chuckled when she learned that her husband, Lee Hamilton, had agreed to be a part of this then-and-now look at some of Indiana's most noteworthy former high school basketball players. Mrs. Hamilton said it was kind of funny that whenever her husband is introduced at a political dinner, the emcee will not only include several of the Congressman's most notable accomplishments in government service, but invariably will squeeze in the fact he is in the Indiana Basketball Hall of Fame.

"My wife was probably joking about the Indiana Hall of Fame," said Hamilton. "If anybody introduces you, they'll look over your resume and see all this, that, and the other, which doesn't mean anything to them. They almost will invariably cite the Indiana Basketball Hall of Fame. Indiana, of course, is famous for basketball.

"I always joke about it, because the night I was inducted they brought in Bobby Knight and Oscar Robertson. I was in distinguished company. The emcee was making a presentation to Oscar, and said that during his NBA career he scored whatever it was, 26,000 points [26,710 to be exact]. The emcee was a friend of mine, and I turned to him and said, 'Just forget my point total, please.'"

Since leaving the House of Representatives, Hamilton has continued to score points in government service. He is the director of the Woodrow Wilson International Center for Scholars in Washington, D.C., and director of the Center on Congress at Indiana University. Hamilton also served on the 9/11 Commission.

Although he doesn't have time to see as many basketball games as he'd like, Hamilton remains a sports fan. He said, "I've had a good friendship with a lot of the writers over the years, some of it relating to politics and some to sports. I'm an avid reader of the sports pages. I guess maybe a little less so than I used to be, but I still read them very carefully. I begin the day looking at the sports pages."

Born in Daytona Beach, Florida, Hamilton didn't become interested in basketball until the family moved to Evansville when he was in eighth grade. He immediately fell in love with the sport.

"You remember the movie *Hoosiers*," he said. "My experience was very similar to that, only with a larger school, not a small school; but it became kind of the center of things for me."

As a junior and senior at Evansville Central, Hamilton made a lot of sports news, along with teammate Gene Southwood, who was an Indiana All-Star in 1948.

"We had very, very good teams my last two years of high school," said Hamilton. "In my junior year, we got put out of the tournament in the Bloomington semifinal by Clyde Lovellette and Ronnie Bland of Terre Haute Garfield [in the championship game]. In my senior year we were undefeated throughout most of the season. We got beat in the final game of the regular season in Bedford, then went to the final game of the tournament."

Hamilton was a 6-foot-3 center, "small nowadays," he says. The Bears rallied to beat Muncie Central, 48-40, in the afternoon, but Hamilton severely hurt his right knee toward the end of the game. "I could not finish the game," he said. "We had a great fan, [Dr. Gilbert Hyatt], who traveled with us, and he happened to be an orthopedic physician. He took me down to the bowels of Butler Fieldhouse and looked at my knee. He knew it was a fairly serious problem. I had torn a cartilage."

The doctor began to maneuver the knee around to get it back in place. "That's a fairly painful process," said Hamilton, "and when they do that they usually give you some kind of anesthetic, but they didn't want to do that in my case. The doctor got the cartilage in place and bandaged the knee heavily and put a splint on it. He told the coach we could try it for the night game, but I don't know how long it will last."

Hamilton started against Lafayette Jeff, a team the Bears had beaten pretty decisively during a holiday tournament at Lafayette (65-51). After several minutes of the first quarter, Hamilton hurt the knee again. "It was clear, the doctor said, they couldn't fix it," he said. "I spent the rest of the game down on a training table listening to it on the radio. They were televising the game, but didn't have it on in the locker room. And we got beat [54-42]."

Hamilton might be the only recipient of the coveted Trester Award for mental attitude to receive it in the dressing room. "The award was actually given to my father, who stepped out onto the floor to receive it," he said. "He brought it down to the locker room."

That must have been a bittersweet moment, to which Hamilton replied, "It was more bitter than sweet at the moment for me. We had lost the game, and quite frankly, all of us believed it was a team we could beat, because we had done it during the regular season. Gene Southwood and I were the key scorers. We worked very well together. And my injury kind of discombobulated our entire offense and defense."

Winning the Trester Award has taken on new meaning for Hamilton. "At the time I was awarded the Trester Award I didn't really think all that much about it," he said. "My goal throughout high school was to win the state tournament. We had failed. I was deeply, deeply disappointed. The Trester Award was kind of a runner-up prize, I guess. I didn't appreciate the significance of it, to be frank about it, at the time it was given to me. Over the years, given the prestige of the award in the sate, of course my attitude began to change. I recognized what a great honor it was to receive."

Hamilton had a number of college scholarship offers. The one he considered most seriously was to Vanderbilt, where Southwood went, but Hamilton's family favored DePauw and that's where he enrolled on a Rector Scholarship, which paid most of his educational expenses.

"It was not an easy decision for my family, because I had a free ride at Vanderbilt, and we were not a well-to-do family," said Hamilton. "I went to

DePauw, and made a decision not to move ahead with big-time basketball. We were very good my first three years. We always played a couple of Big Ten schools and got beat by 'em.

"At that time they had a tournament for smaller schools, and I always was disappointed DePauw University didn't let us play in that, even though we had invitations to them. We had a very poor season my senior year. It was the only year I played that we did not do well. That was a bit of a shock to me, because I had never been on a team like that before."

After his DePauw days, Hamilton had professional offers from teams in Fort Wayne and Oklahoma, but opted to go into law school at Indiana University in Bloomington. Any regrets about not turning pro?

"If the context were today," he said, "I'd have gone ahead, because you earn so much money even if you sit on the bench, but that was not the case back then. In those days, the pro game was very tough. Bangin' around on buses. It was not a very attractive life. I wasn't that high up, and I was only offered a few thousand dollars. I don't even remember being indecisive about it. You naturally wonder how you would have done, but you do that every time you make a decision in life."

After a year of study in Germany, Hamilton went to Indiana University, where he earned a law degree in 1956. He practiced in Chicago and Columbus, Indiana, until finally deciding to run for Congress in 1964. "Basically I was bored practicing law," said Hamilton.

Hamilton remains a faithful fan of Hoosier Hysteria. "You bet I am," he exclaimed. "I promote it all the time."

Mark Herrmann

Central High School, Carmel

Year graduated
1977

Major accomplishments
Received the Trester Award for mental attitude; Ended college career
with nine NCAA records, including 9,188 passing yards in football;
A fourth-round draft choice in 1981 by Denver

Mark Herrmann is a football man—always has been, always will be. Nevertheless, the former Purdue All-America quarterback, 11-year NFL performer, and current Indianapolis Colts radio analyst also was a pretty good basketball player. Good enough, in fact, to help the Carmel Greyhounds win their only state high school championship.

The year was 1977, and the 6-foot-4 Herrmann and his starting buddies, Bart Burrell, Jon Ogle, Tim Wiley, and Paul Hensel; all of who had been together since they were undefeated in the seventh grade; were unranked and huge underdogs in the title game against East Chicago Washington. Carmel defied the odds, and before a capacity crowd of 17,490 in Indianapolis' Market Square Arena, upset the Senators, 53-52, in what Herb Schwomeyer described in his *Hoosier Hysteria* book as "one of the most inspiring final-game performances since Milan's Cinderella team shocked highly favored Muncie Central in 1954."

Herrmann says his team was probably a double-digit underdog, at least, against East Chicago. "We had watched them in the afternoon game, and they looked awfully impressive. They beat Terre Haute South pretty handily [66-45]. We knew we had to beat Columbus East to get to the championship game. We played very well, and won by double digits [71-60]. Although East Chicago was a prohibitive favorite at night, we thought, 'Hey, if we play our game, who knows what could happen.' We had played a 2-3 zone the whole tournament and we stuck with that. We executed very well and frustrated them a little bit."

After Carmel took a sizeable lead in the third quarter, East Chicago rallied and grabbed a 52-51 lead on Morris' two free throws with 11 seconds to play. That's when the real drama began during a Carmel timeout.

"Coach [Eric] Clark said, 'Let's get the ball into Mark and let him take the last shot,'" said Herrmann. "I couldn't get open. Morris and I went for the ball on the in-bounds pass. The refs couldn't decide who touched the ball last and called for a jump ball."

During that Carmel timeout, Burrell, who became one of Herrmann's top receivers at Purdue, tried to fire up his team. "The year before we had lost in the state football championship game to Valparaiso by one point," said Herrmann. "So Bart said, 'Let's not lose another one-point game.'"

On the jump ball between Herrmann and Morris at the Senators' end of the floor, Burrell made the play of the game. "Bart had kinda figured out where Drake was going to tip the ball most of the day, and I think he figured Drake would get the tip. Bart said, 'Everybody out of the way,' and Drake tipped the ball back right to him. He took it on the run, and threw about a half-court alley-oop pass to Ogle. Jon laid it in with four seconds left. It was a heckuva pass and a great shot."

Morris took a last-second shot that would have won the game for East Chicago, but it missed, giving Herrmann and buddies a championship victory.

"We were hugging and tears were streaming down our faces," said Herrmann. "We had five senior starters, and we had been together a very long time."

Morris, who went to Purdue on a basketball scholarship, had 37 points against Terre Haute South and 27 against Carmel. He made the Indiana All-Star team. None of the other Greyhounds were voted onto the team. Herrmann, who had 22 points against Columbus East, and 16 against East Chicago, plus six rebounds and six assists, considers that a compliment for a group that played as a unit.

"There wasn't a star on the team," he said. "Nobody went on to play Division I ball, which is unheard of these days. I think the fact that we had no All-Stars was something to be very proud of.

"When my family moved to Carmel from Kansas City, which was more of a football town, in my sixth grade year, I got exposed to basketball and loved it. I wish Indiana high school basketball was still like it was, one class, because that was a tremendous thing the state of Indiana had to be proud of. I think some of the small schools miss having that opportunity to knock off the big schools. Coming from 13-7 at the end of the regular season in '77, nobody gave us a chance. I think that made it even sweeter winning a state championship."

Herrmann still has three mementos from that game he treasures: a piece of the championship net, a championship ring, and the Trester Award trophy. "It was like a cherry on top of the sundae to be singled out for such a prestigious award," he said.

Of Carmel's 14-13 loss to Valparaiso in the '76 state football championship game, Herrmann said, "To fall short was devastating, because we felt we had the best team in the state by far. The week before we had beaten a very good Richmond team in 70-degree weather in Butler Bowl. Then we had to go up to Valpo and play in 20-degree weather at night. We missed an extra point to tie it, and lost."

In his freshman year at Purdue, Herrmann says it was brought up that he might play two sports. Herrmann opted to concentrate on football, and it paid off big-time. In four seasons as a starter, he led the Boilermakers to a 33-13-1 record and bowl victories his last three years: Peach, Bluebonnet, and Liberty. Herrmann, who finished fourth in Heisman Trophy voting as a senior, ended his career with nine NCAA records, including 9,188 regular-season major-college passing yards.

"I got to play all four years, and we threw the ball a lot," he said of his Boilermaker days. "A Rose Bowl would have been nice, but I had a lot of great teammates and some good memories."

A fourth-round pick by Denver in the 1981 NFL draft, Herrmann wound up playing for five different teams: The Broncos, Baltimore, San Diego, the Los Angeles Rams, and the Indianapolis Colts. He calls his pro career good and bad.

"I was fortunate to play a lot of years, which beats the average," he said. "The average is about three years. I was more of a backup most of my career.

That was a little frustrating and disappointing, but to have had a chance to play at the highest level was a great thrill. I had my share of good games, but not enough."

Ironically, Herrmann's career ended the day after he led the Colts to victory in 1992 in one of his best games.

"I was offensive player of the game, got the game ball, went home to our neighborhood and had a nice celebration," he said. "It was the first time the Colts had won a home opener since they moved to Indianapolis from Baltimore."

His excitement quickly turned to shock the next morning. Before he could begin lifting weights, Herrmann was called to owner Jim Irsay's office. "He said, 'A great win yesterday. You played a great game. But we're going to have to release you.' In their minds they felt like they had to go with some other players. We shook hands and I walked out of his office, and that was it, never to step on a football field again. People still talk about that to this day. I had the entire media of the city in my front yard when I got home. It was quite a circus. You go from Cloud Nine one day, then out of a job the next."

Herrmann chose not to "blast everybody," and he's glad he took the professional approach, because "I really enjoy doing radio for the Colts games" and his position as associate director of education programs with the NCAA, which he assumed four years ago.

"We have a program called Stay in Bounds, which is a character development program," said Herrmann. "I was one of the volunteer speakers for the program, in which former athletes talk to school groups about their experiences in sports, highs and lows. There was an opening, and I was approached about filling it. It's a position that I've enjoyed."

Mike McCoy

Fort Wayne South High School, Fort Wayne

Year graduated
1958

Major accomplishments
Had the most points (86) over the final four games of the 1958
tournament; Mr. Basketball; Honorable mention All-America in 1962
and '63 at the University of Miami; Won the national AAU tournament
in 1964 and '67, the U.S. Olympic Trials in '64, and the World Cup in
1966 in Rome; Indiana Basketball Hall of Famer

Long before the Lawrence North Wildcats had Greg Oden, a national
phenomenon, there was Mike McCoy, the first 7-footer in Indiana
high school basketball history to lead a team to the state
championship.

"When they wrote the little bio for my induction into the Indiana
Basketball Hall of Fame in 1993, it said, 'Mike McCoy, Indiana's first
intimidating big man,'" said the '58 Mr. Basketball. "I kinda liked that."

After South defeated Elkhart, 76-44, to win the Fort Wayne semistate
in '58, the Elkhart coach was asked what went wrong. He replied, "My boys
had McCoy-itis." The lopsided victory sent the Archers to Butler Fieldhouse
(now Hinkle Fieldhouse) in Indianapolis for the state finals against
Crawfordsville, Muncie Central, and Springs Valley.

Although South had beat 10 opponents on the way to the state
championship by an average of 19.3 points, they had trouble with Springs
Valley in the morning round. Nevertheless, they won, 55-42. Crawfordsville
beat Muncie Central, 53-45, in the other morning game.

"Springs Valley was 28-0," recalled McCoy, who still meets with many of the starters on his former Archers the first Monday of every month at the Acme bar in Fort Wayne. "They had five unbelievably tough kids. I'm talkin' scrappy. We ended up beating them 13 points, but early in the first quarter there was a fellow guarding me who would pinch the back of my legs and hang onto my pants. I got a pass, pivoted, and caught him flush in the nose with my left elbow. He didn't bother me the rest of the game."

McCoy has a picture showing four Springs Valley players pointing at him as he finished a jump shot, believing that McCoy threw an elbow on purpose. Did McCoy throw the elbow on purpose? "Yes, of course; he was bothering me, but I never got called for the foul," he said. "I think it changed the tempo of the game."

During the Silver Anniversary celebration of that '58 state finals in 1983, McCoy was watching film of the South/Springs Valley game with a group of former players. Just as the action showed him beginning his game-turning pivot, he turned to a fellow Indiana All-Star, Edgar Searcy of Indianapolis Crispus Attucks, and said, "That guy was bothering the hell out of me. I had to give him an elbow in the nose to get him off my back. I don't remember his name."

A fellow standing next to McCoy said, "That was me." It was Bob McCracken, another Indiana All-Star.

The Athenians' morning victory over the Bearcats was a warning for the Archers. "They kicked Muncie Central's butt," said McCoy. "We couldn't believe it. We thought, 'Where did this team come from?'"

South led by a scant margin at halftime, prompting coach Don Reichert to give his team "a good talking-to." The Archers turned their 1-3-1 zone into high gear in the second half, and wound up winning by one of the most lopsided margins in tournament history.

"Don was death on fundamentals—blocking out and good defense," said McCoy, who had over 50 rebounds and a ton of blocked shots in the tournament. "We didn't run and shoot, we worked the ball. Years later, when I thought about it, I realized that for the personnel Don had, what a great defense our 1-3-1 zone was. You had Rich Miller chasing out front, Tom Bolyard, Carl Stavreti, and me across the center, and Dan Howe running the baseline."

Few Indiana players had to clear more hurdles on their way to stardom than McCoy. If it hadn't been for Reichert, McCoy might have faded into athletic obscurity.

"When I was inducted into the hall of fame, the last thing I did in my speech was to thank several people, and thank Don Reichert," he said. "I said something to the effect, 'Don taught a lot of kids a lot of things about basketball, but most of all he taught a lot of kids how to live their lives, and he did it by example. Don Reichert was probably one of the straightest, most honest, most inspiring people I've ever met. He was tough as hell out on the floor and in the locker room, but he was right down the middle."

McCoy's only sibling, older brother Gene, was about 6-foot-9 and 360 pounds when he played football one year at South. He became self-conscious about his size and quit school, going to work for an uncle at McCoy Boat Works. "Gene later went back and finished school after he got married," said McCoy. "But he wasn't prepared for the talk, jokes, this, that, and the other thing regarding his size."

McCoy was far more fortunate in being accepted as a tall basketball player. "I went to St. Pete's Catholic grade school. When I graduated from St. Pete's in 1954, I was 6-foot-3. Bill Hicks stopped by the house a couple of times to try and get me to go to Central Catholic High School.

"But because my brother was already at South, I decided to go there. When I started in September, I was 6-foot-9. I grew six inches in three months. Needless to say I spent a lot of time in bed, because the strain was just unbelievable. When I showed a little bit of promise as a freshman, I was accepted by all the kids from the public schools, who probably felt we were going to be together for the next four years and that I was going to be a little bit different from the rest of the kids. That made the transition easier."

In the seventh grade at St. Peter's, McCoy was cut from the basketball team. He was told by the coach he would never amount to anything in basketball, and that he should try another sport. He told himself he was going to come back and try the next year, "Which I did," said McCoy. "I had a different coach, and it just sort of went from there."

McCoy broke a foot and missed his sophomore season. "I could have quit school if it had not been for Don Reichert," he said. "I was on crutches, and he came and made sure I got to school. I was really discouraged, but I hung in there."

McCoy missed the first half of his junior season because of grades. South was 6-foot-6 when he returned to the lineup. "We never lost another game until South Bend Central, which went 30-0 and won the state championship, beat us," said McCoy.

Earning the Mr. Basketball tag for the Indiana All-Stars surprised McCoy, who thought the honor might go to Terry Dischinger Terre Haute or Charlie Hall of Searcy. "Although I led our team in scoring my junior and senior years, I only averaged about 18 points a game. When I learned I was going to be named Mr. Basketball, I was overwhelmed. It was quite an honor, but it wasn't as big of an honor as winning the state championship."

On McCoy's way to the University of Miami during the second half of the 1958-59 college basketball season, he nearly froze to death in Evanston, Illinois, site of Northwestern University.

"The appeal of Northwestern was Chicago," said McCoy. "I didn't realize it was going to be so cold up there."

During Christmas break, McCoy returned to Fort Wayne and spent time with the Stavreti brothers, Chris and Carl. Chris, who graduated from South in 1957, had been offered a scholarship to Miami by coach Bruce Hale. McCoy asked Chris how he liked it in Miami and the reply was, "The campus is beautiful and the weather is out of this world." To which McCoy replied, "If you don't mind, I'll probably go back with you. I didn't realize what a plus that was gonna be.

"When I got of high school I weighed 200 pounds. But by the time I got to my sophomore year at Miami I was going about 250. I did a lot of weight work and I was very strong. I loved the run-and-shoot offense and man-to-man defense Hale used. We had unbelievably good times, and we had good basketball teams. When I got to my senior year, we had Rick Barry and Carl [Stavreti], and we had one helluva good team."

McCoy was honorable mention All-America in 1962 and '63, and then was drafted in the top 25 by the Detroit Pistons. In the meantime, he was invited to play for the Marion Kay Spices team of Brownstown, Indiana, in the national AAU tournament in Denver. Shortly thereafter he was invited to Akron, Ohio, to talk with Hank Vaughn, coach of the Goodyears in the National Industrial Basketball League. McCoy learned he could make around $10,000 a year playing basketball and working in management for the company. That was the amount he would have received from the Pistons had he decided to play in the NBA, so he joined the Goodyears.

In his four NIBL seasons, the Goodyears won the national AAU tournament in 1964 and '67, the Olympics Trials in '64, and the World Cup in 1966 in Rome. "Let me tell you what kind of a team we had," said McCoy. "After winning the 1964 national AAU tournament, we were selected to represent the AAU in the Olympic Trials in St. John's Arena in New York. We played UCLA, John Wooden's first national championship team that was undefeated, and we beat 'em by 23 points. I wasn't that much of a force, but Larry Brown, Dick Davies, and Pete McCaffrey were selected from our team for the Olympic squad that won a gold medal in Tokyo."

McCoy remained with Goodyear for 21 years, then went into sales and marketing in chemical supplies in Detroit, working there until he moved back to Fort Wayne in 1997 with his second wife, Helen, who is 5 feet tall. McCoy had no children by his first wife, but Helen has two. "Hopefully I helped do something to raise them," he said. "They turned out great." The couple shares four grandchildren.

McCoy is happy to be back in his hometown. He says his wife feels like being in Fort Wayne is "going back to the Fifties. She was born and raised in New York City, then lived in Connecticut, so for her it's a little bit of a cultural shock out here. We constantly run into people who come up and ask about my sport. Her answer to that is, 'Don't these people ever get on with their lives? How can they remember details of something that happened 50 years ago?' I try to tell her that's Indiana basketball."

Joe Sexson

Tech High School, Indianapolis

Year graduated
1952

Major accomplishments
Received Trester Award for mental attitude; Named Mr. Basketball;
On the IHSAA Silver Anniversary team in 1977; Indiana Basketball
Hall of Famer; Indianapolis Public Schools Hall of Famer

As Joe Sexson, 72, sat in the home west of Zionsville, Indiana, which he shares with his wife of 53 years, Donna, he laughed often while describing what happened during a basketball game at Kokomo his senior year at Tech, a game won by the Wildkats.

"They didn't care much for me up there," said Sexson. "They had a very good team. In fact, they and Muncie Central were the two best teams we played all year. At the time, I was the guy at Tech, and we were in the North Central Conference at the same time.

"I'll tell you how rabid [the fans] were. My grandmother hardly went to any games, but she went to that one. A person was getting after me, I guess, and she finally hit him on the head, I think, with her purse." Sexson laughed uproariously, then added, "If you knew my grandmother, you'd know she never did that. So it must have been pretty bad. But I think they were just rabid fans. After the game, here's how bad they were from that standpoint, and it didn't bother me at all. Some little kid, which I've always liked young kids, came up to me. His mother came up and said, 'Come here, honey, get away from him, he'll grab you or he'll take you away. Yeah, he'll steal you,' or something."

That game might have triggered the telegram sent from Kokomo to the late IHSAA commissioner, L.V. Phillips, protesting the selection of Sexson for the Trester Award. Kokomo school officials and student body representatives later sent apologies to the IHSAA and Sexson.

"I don't know that I did anything to cause them to feel that way," said Sexson, "but there must have been a group or it might gave been one guy who wrote in. I don't know." Sexson says it didn't detract from his award.

Sports weren't specialized the way they are today when Sexson was growing up on Indianapolis' south side. He earned 13 letters at Tech: four in baseball and three each in football, basketball and track. In baseball, Sexson played the outfield and shortstop, in football left halfback and on defense, in basketball center at 6-foot-3, and in track he ran the 100 and 220.

"My track coach, Paul Myers, wanted me to give up the other sports and concentrate on track," said Sexson. "He thought I could be an Olympian, but I didn't do it. I just wanted to keep having a good time playing all the other sports."

Sexson remembers a football game against Richmond when the Red Devils had Lamar Lundy, Jimmy Peters, and Dick Murley, all of whom went to Purdue. "We ran a fake reverse," said Sexson. "They centered the ball to me, and I took it toward the right halfback, faked it to him, then was going around end. And there was Lundy. Needless to say, he swallowed me up."

As a sophomore, Sexson's Tech basketball team "ran into Spence Schnaitter and the Madison state champs. Madison beat us, 55-46, in the semifinals. In '52 we got beat in the final game by Danny Thornburg and the Muncie Bearcats," when the North Central Conference "was very good. Tech is no longer in that conference."

That loss was a big disappointment, says Sexson. "You get to the final game you want to win the state championship. But [the Bearcats] were just too quick for us and too good. In fact, they had beaten us 19 during the regular season, then 19 again in the final game."

Receiving the Trester Award for mental attitude and being named Mr. Basketball for the Indiana All-Star team were very meaningful to Sexson. He does think "the Trester Award has been watered down now. We have a Trester Award in every division in basketball, but I am sure it means a whole lot to each young man."

Of the chance for small-town teams to stand on the winners' stand in class basketball, Sexson says, "I think it's wonderful for those young kids in the different classes, very honestly. The reason I think that is because of everything I've read, and everything I see now when I see the championship games. Those kids are so excited and feel so good about winning."

After leaving Tech, Sexson talked to several Big Ten schools. He made a visit to Indiana, and spent the weekend with Dick Farley, a member of the Hoosiers' 1953 NCAA championship team. He even pledged a fraternity.

"But after I thought about it, I felt Purdue gave me the best opportunity to play earlier," said Sexson. "That's the reason I went to Purdue."

Sexson went out for football as a Boilermaker freshman, but he wasn't allowed to practice until he had a hernia repaired. Sexson decided to leave the gridiron and concentrate on basketball and baseball.

"My years at Purdue were just great," he said. "Unfortunately, we didn't win any championships. I got to travel a lot, and we played in the Big Ten, which was very competitive." Sexson set a career scoring record of 1,095 points in basketball that has been broken several times since (the career record of 2,323 is now held by Rick Mount).

On the day Sexson graduated from Purdue, he and Donna flew to Detroit to work out for the Tigers. While there, he hit a baseball out of the old Tiger Stadium. The Tigers wanted to sign him to a contract, but he says he didn't have a strong arm. "I was gonna have to be a first baseman. I assume that's why they wanted to start me real low. At that time they weren't paying that much, and I didn't see any future there." Sexson was also drafted by the NBA's Knicks, but never went to New York.

Instead, he took a job coaching and teaching at Southwestern High School, a new consolidation near Lafayette, Indiana. He was there a year, then spent two years coaching and teaching at Scecina High School in Indianapolis. From there, Sexson returned to his alma mater, and spent 18 years as assistant basketball coach and head baseball coach.

Purdue finished runner-up to UCLA in the 1969 NCAA basketball tournament, and won the NIT in 1974 when Sexson was on the staff. "We had Terry Dischinger, along with Rick Mount, and they were probably the outstanding players at the time I was there, along with Frank Kendrick. Frank was really hot at the time we won the NIT."

After the 1976-77 college basketball season, Sexson got a phone call from Bill Sylvester, Butler athletic director. "He was looking for a coach," said Sexson, "and it didn't look like I was going to get to be the head coach at Purdue, so I went to Butler and had 12 great years."

Sexson was 143-188 with the Bulldogs, the Indiana Collegiate Conference coach of the year in 1978, and Midwestern Collegiate Conference coach of the year in 1984. Sexson's 1984-85 team (19-10) played Indiana in the NIT at Bloomington. IU won, 79-57.

"Bobby Knight was very nice," said Sexson. Laughing, he added, "Of course, he beat us. I loved the kids on our team and was looking forward to going to IU to play that game, until I found out that every one of the kids that was playing for me had wanted to go to IU"

"Chad Tucker was the best all-around player I had at Butler," said Sexson. "Darrin Fitzgerald, [NCAA record-holder for three-pointers in a season with 158 in 1986-87], was the best shooter I had. I never thought in coaching I would set blocks out that high for a guy to shoot the ball. But he could shoot that three-pointer from a mile away."

After leaving Butler in 1989, Sexson and Donna, also a Tech graduate, bought the Big Pine golf course in Attica, Indiana. They kept it five years, then retired. The couple has three sons and nine grandchildren.

George Crowe

Franklin High School, Franklin

Year graduated
1939

Major accomplishments
**Mr. Basketball; Indiana All-Star; Indiana Basketball Hall of Famer;
Indiana Baseball Hall of Famer**

In 1989, to commemorate the 50th anniversary of the Indiana-Kentucky All-Star series, *The Indianapolis Star*, sponsor of the event, presented golden basketballs to the living members of its first All-Star team during a reception in the Indiana Convention Center at Indianapolis.

It was the first, and only time, golden basketballs have been given to former Indiana All-Stars. The players on that first All-Star team in 1939 were George Crowe of Franklin, Indiana's first Mr. Basketball; George Fields, Mooresville; Don Frazier, Greencastle; Bud Goodwin, Bloomington; Fred Krampe, Indianapolis Shortridge; Roger Bundy, Salem; Wayne Payton, Spencer; George Taylor, Greencastle; John Williams, Indianapolis Southport; and Howard Mitchell, Indianapolis Attucks.

That first Indiana All-Star team played coach Everett Case's state high school championship team, the Frankfort Hotdogs, on August 18, 1939, in Butler Fieldhouse (now Hinkle Fieldhouse). The All-Stars won, 31-21, and for Crowe, who later became the first African American from Indiana to play Major League Baseball, it was a game of redemption.

Crowe, younger brother of the late Ray Crowe who coached Attucks to state championships in 1955 and '56, led Franklin to the state finals in '39.

Despite the fact that Crowe scored 13 points on six field goals and a free throw, the Cubs lost to Frankfort, 36-22, in the championship game before a crowd of 14,983.

In that game, Franklin and Frankfort were tied, 5-5, at the end of the first quarter. But according to one newspaper account at the time, "From the opening minute of the second quarter on, the Hot Dogs [sic] took complete control of the game and tied up the Cubs with the exception of Crowe, Franklin's great colored center who proved to be the best individual player in the tournament. He contributed 13 points to Franklin's cause, and in addition to playing a bang-up game on offense turned in some beautiful work on defense."

Crowe was named center on the *Indianapolis News*' all-state team of 1939. Bill Fox, the *News* sports editor then, wrote of Crowe: "I saw two games of the Tech semi-final tournament and the three games in the [Butler] Fieldhouse . . . and where I sat George Crowe, Franklin's center, was the tournament's outstanding player. And according to a good old *News* custom the word tournament applies to the last sixteen teams in the field of 779. Richly endowed physically and tutored in his court knowledge by the greatest individual performer as well as team man that this state has ever produced [that's Fuzzy, you know], George Crowe carried the fight at night as he did in the afternoon when Franklin won from those [Muncie] Burris Owls, 31 to 25."

Fuzzy, of course, referred to Robert "Fuzzy" Vandivier, the coach of that '39 Franklin team. Vandivier, who helped the Cubs become known as the Franklin "Wonder Five" by becoming the first team to win three consecutive state titles in 1920, '21 and '22, called Crowe "the best money player I ever saw."

The '39 state tournament championship game brought together two teams that had won three titles. A Franklin victory would have given Vandivier, who is in both the Indiana and National Basketball Halls of Fame, four championships, three as a player and one as a coach. Case, who also is in the Indiana and National Halls of Fame, beat him to No. 4. He earlier had won titles as the Frankfort coach in 1925, 1929 and 1936.

It was that same that *The Star* decided to showcase Indiana All-Stars in competition during the summer following the state tournament (Kentucky became Indiana's opponent in 1940). The first two Indiana teams were selected by a popular vote of fans in the state. Crowe won Mr. Basketball in a landslide, and even though his statistics in the first All-Star game weren't awesome by today's standards, he did the honor proud.

The Star published a history of the All-Star series during that golden anniversary year. In describing the first game, in which the Indiana All-Stars held Frankfort scoreless in the third quarter, the late Don Bates of *The Star* wrote: "Franklin's George Crowe, the first Mr. Basketball, was the All-Stars' most effective defense weapon. Playing in the middle, he repeatedly denied inside access to the basket and forced Frankfort to take lower-percentage shots. Crowe hauled in 10 rebounds and scored five points in helping the All-Stars out-rebound the taller Hotdogs."

From 1940 through 1954 a single All-Star game was played in Indianapolis. A home-and-home format with Kentucky was begun in 1955. A girls' series was started in 1976. In 1941, the balloting process was changed to include only sportswriters and broadcasters throughout the state. In 1978, voting was expanded to include sportswriters, broadcasters, and coaches.

If fate hadn't smiled on him, Crowe might never have become Mr. Basketball. Crowe didn't participate in competitive sports until he was a junior at Franklin High School.

"I didn't even try out," he said, "because they never had any black players, you know? Other guys who were good enough, they weren't allowed to play."

Crowe got the opportunity to represent his school when a new junior varsity basketball coach arrived at Franklin High. "I was in his gym class," said Crowe. "He saw me play and told me to come out for his team. So I went out and made the team, and after a while we practiced against the varsity. We beat 'em pretty good. The next day, I was promoted to the varsity basketball team."

In the late '30s and early '40s, opportunities in sports were limited for blacks. Like his older brothers Ray and Richard, Crowe enrolled at Indiana Central College [now the University of Indianapolis] after graduating from Franklin High. He became a star in basketball, baseball, and track for the school on the southside of Indianapolis, and he was inducted into the Greyhound Club Hall of Fame in 1986.

After earning a degree in physical education, Crowe went into the army and served as a first lieutenant in a segregated unit in the quartermaster corps in Asia. When he returned home, Crowe played professional basketball for seven years with the Los Angeles Red Devils, New York Renaissance and the Harlem Yankees.

In 1947 Crowe played for the New York Black Yankees baseball team in the Negro National League. A year later the Black Yankees team went broke, but by then Branch Rickey had broken Major League Baseball's color barrier by signing Jackie Robinson to a Brooklyn Dodgers contract.

The Boston (now Atlanta) Braves invited Crowe to spring training, and the 6-foot-3, 212-pound first baseman was impressive enough to earn a minor league contract. Crowe played for ten years in the major leagues with the Milwaukee Braves before they moved to Atlanta, the Cincinnati Reds, and St. Louis Cardinals. He retired in 1961.

During his major leagues years, Crowe fell in love with the Catskill Mountains in New York, and after retirement spent 11 years in a one-room log cabin without electricity, running water, or central heating. He later returned to a regular house in Long Eddy, New York.

Crowe once said he regretted that he didn't get to play enough when he was young. "That's one of those born too soon things," he added, but quickly stated, "I had fun during my time."

He also has golden memories. He was selected to play in the 1958 Major League All-Star game, in addition to being inducted into the Indiana Basketball Hall of Fame in 1976 and the Indiana Baseball Hall of Fame in 2004. In his honor, the Franklin High School baseball field was named Crowe Field.

Sean May

Bloomington North High School, Bloomington

Year graduated
2002

Major accomplishments
Mr. Basketball; Named MVP for Final Four

Sean May was born in Chicago, but spent the majority of his first few years in Italy with his parents while his father played professional basketball. May took up the tradition, and currently plays professional basketball with the NBA's Bobcats in Charlotte, North Carolina, not far from Chapel Hill where he made University of North Carolina fans happy on his 21st birthday by leading the Tar Heels to the 2005 NCAA championship.

In between those extremes, Sean, a Sandusky, Ohio, native who led Indiana University to the 1976 NCAA title with a perfect 32-0 record, became an adopted Hoosier after his father retired from the pro game and returned to Bloomington, Indiana, to live permanently when May was just five.

"My mom lived in Italy with my dad, but she didn't like the hospital there, so she came back to Chicago to have me," said May, whose father spent five seasons with the Chicago Bulls of the NBA, and one season each with Milwaukee and Detroit before going to Italy.

"We came back to Bloomington every year after the season ended in Italy, then we'd go back to Italy for the new season. I grew up watching Indiana basketball ever since I was young, and I have to consider myself a Hoosier."

The basketball bug bites many Indiana kids at a very early age. It wasn't that way with May. He didn't even watch the tape of his father's NCAA championship game until after his freshman year in college.

"I knew my father was a helluva player, but he didn't really work with me much until I was going into my sophomore season at Bloomington North High School," said May. "He didn't want to put too much pressure on me.

"Everything came natural to me in Bloomington. My feel for the game came from watching tape and talking to my father. I don't want to say that I didn't work on certain things, but nothing out of the ordinary. I just did a lot more than probably a lot of kids do."

As a sophomore at Bloomington North in 2000, the Cougars went all the way to the state championship game undefeated at 25-0. Before a sellout crowd of 18,263 in Conseco Fieldhouse in Indianapolis, they met the 27-1 Marion Giants. North was rated No. 1, Marion No. 2 in Indiana. However, in a *USA Today* poll, North was ranked No. 20 while Marion was at No. 6.

Marion, with Zach Randolph scoring 28 points and grabbing nine rebounds, defeated North, 62-56, to claim its seventh title. May was North's high scorer with 17 points, but none came after intermission.

When asked what happened, May offered no excuses. "They just did a good job of adjusting to our game plan," he said. "I was young and probably wasn't as aggressive as I should be. I just didn't play well.

"But it was great game. We probably could have won that game had we played just a little bit better. It was a great experience to play against Zach. There were three future NBA players on that court. I don't think you can get that a lot of times in any other state."

Of that disappointing title game, May says, "Through college that was one of my main motivations for winning a college championship, because I didn't win one in high school. I came so close. I think we were all caught up in the nerve [in 2000], and for us to go 25-0 and lose that last game, that's probably one of the most difficult things I've ever been through."

When May was a senior at North, he was named Mr. Basketball and helped Indiana win a pair of games versus Kentucky in their All-Star rivalry in 2002. May had 49 points in the two games, and scored 30 in an 87-82 victory at Owensboro, Kentucky.

"Being Mr. Basketball means a lot," he said, "because you think about the guys who won that award, going all the way back to Damon Bailey, Luke Recker, Jason Gardner, Chris Thomas, and Jared when it could have been a question of him or Zach. There have been a lot of guys who I know, and have played against, and seen who have won that award. So for me to come up in Indiana and see those guys and see Indiana basketball, it's a great accomplishment."

Early in May's career at North, he went to Assembly Hall on the Indiana University campus, where his father led the Hoosiers and coach Bob Knight to a 63-1 record in the 1974-75 and 1975-76 seasons, to play in pickup games.

"There's a lot of good competition there," he said. "I had a great relationship with Coach Knight. When you're in high school you can't really talk to college coaches that much. But had he been at Indiana when I graduated I was going to be there. I almost committed [to Indiana] right after my freshman year [at North], just because I knew I didn't want to go through the recruiting process. It was going to be Indiana, but that's when he got in all that trouble [and was fired on September 10, 2000]."

May was later quoted as saying he didn't want to try to be another Scott May in Bloomington. "My whole thing with that was my dad's legacy at Indiana is pretty big for what he did and what they accomplished. I wouldn't have minded that pressure, but not playing for the same coach [Knight] I felt that pressure would be unwarranted. It wouldn't be the same. If Coach Knight would have been there I'd have loved to have attempted to live up to that [legacy], but I felt once Coach Knight left it was an opportunity for me to go and do my own thing and make my own legacy somewhere else."

Every major school in the country went after May. He narrowed his choices to North Carolina and Louisville. "I visited both of them. I just fell in love with North Carolina, the history, everything they have there, the players coming back every year."

Life as a Tar Heel was not an instant success, however. "I had a rocky start," said May. "I broke my foot as a freshman. But I had a pretty good sophomore year, averaging 15 [points] and 10 [rebounds]. In my last year as a junior I flourished, got in better shape and averaged 17 and 11. I just played a lot better."

May credits coach Roy Williams, who replaced former Tar Heel player Matt Doherty after May's freshman year, with helping him realize his huge potential as a 6-foot-9 power forward.

"Coach Williams helped me understand the game, understand what it meant to act like a professional, the way you carry yourself, the way you act in public, the perception you give people of yourself," May said. "And teaching me the game, understanding how to play, understanding the concepts of a team, understanding that you sacrifice yourself for the team."

All of that understanding came to fruition the night of April 4, 2005, in St. Louis when May scored 26 points, and grabbed 10 rebounds in a dominating performance that earned him most valuable player honors in a 75-70 championship victory over Illinois.

"I don't think you'll ever top winning a national title on your 21st birthday," said May. "That night was fun all in its own. Just like any other kid's

21st birthday you go out with your friends and have a good time. Well, for me I was going out with my friends and my teammates after having a good time and winning a national championship. That's an unbelievable feeling and a great accomplishment."

Moments before tip-off that night, May watched a replay of that '76 IU triumph on the Jumbotron. There was a clip of his dad jumping into the arms of teammate Quinn Buckner. He knew something special was about to happen.

"It was an unbelievable feeling," he said, "because I had watched the tape the night before. It was like a sign, that I knew everything was going to be all right, that we were gong to play well. After seeing that and the same feeling I had the night before, how the game was going to go, everything went through my head one last time. It was everything I dreamed about and more. You can't describe those feelings that you have. Only so many people in this world ever know what it's like to win a national championship."

After IU won the 1976 national championship, Scott May appeared on the cover of *Sports Illustrated*, wearing No. 42. After UNC won the 2005 national championship, May was on the cover of *Sports Illustrated*. He, too, was wearing No. 42.

Does May feel in any way one-up on his father? "He's up on me, because he's had a great NBA career, and he's done a little bit more than I have. He taught me everything that I know, so I can't be up on him. We've both been on *Sports Illustrated* covers, and not too many fathers and sons have done that."

Once the 2004-2005 college season ended, May made it clear he wanted to play professionally in Charlotte. "I had a great college career in North Carolina," he said. "The fans in North Carolina have been good to me. It's home for me now. I'm a Tar Heel through and through."

The transplanted Hoosier hopes to wear 42 the rest of his professional career. He's worn that number in honor of his father and Jackie Robinson, whose number was 42 when he became the first American African to play Major League Baseball with the Brooklyn Dodgers.

Hard luck hit on December 23, 2005. In the 23rd game of his NBA rookie season with the Charlotte Bobcats, May suffered an injury to his right knee that ended his season. He averaged 8.2 points.

"It's just like my first year at North Carolina when I broke my foot," he says. "It makes it a learning experience. You can see games from a different perspective."

Epilogue

And now for a postgame wrapup . . .

If Rick Mount had had his druthers, "The Rocket" would not have been the first high school team athlete to appear on the cover of *Sports Illustrated* during the 1965-66 basketball season.

"I was in school [at Lebanon] and [coach Jim Rosenstihl] came to me and said, '*Sports Illustrated* is thinking about doing an article on you,'" said Mount, 1966 Mr. Basketball. "'Put it on the cover.' I said, 'I don't want to do that.' He said, 'Yeah, you are.' Everybody interviewed me, but I wasn't big on talking about myself. I very rarely would talk."

Frank Deford was the writer, and it was one of his first assignments for the magazine. Deford, who went on to become a prize-winning author in many genres, arrived in Lebanon with a crew, recalled Mount. "They're following me around all over school, taking pictures. You know how your peers are; they're standing there making fun of you. The crew was here for two or three weeks."

Mount chuckled, then added, "This is a great story. There was a pool room uptown, on the square. There was a guy named Pistol Sheets—he's in the article. He was a big basketball fan and liked to gamble. We're up on the square and it's on a Friday. Deford and all the *Sports Illustrated* crew are there and we're trying to get in the middle of the street.

"All the farmers are coming into town. It's crowded. It was snowing and there was a lot of slush. We had to get off the street, because here came a lot of cars. Pistol is looking out that window. A few minutes later he comes out and he's got a pistol in his hand. He's waving it and says, 'Rick, I'll stop these cars for you.'

"Deford and all his guys are looking like, 'What have we got ourselves into?' Pistol laughs and goes back in and the guys from *Sports Illustrated* are kinda thinking, 'What's going on?' Then Frank says, 'What was the dip on that?' I said, 'Well, you're in Lebanon, Indiana, you're not in New York now.'"

Mount will never forget the day Rosenstihl told him SI was going to shoot the cover photo north of town. "I said, 'It's snowing and it's cold.' Rosie said, 'Just put these wool warm-ups on over your underwear. You won't be cold.' I took my clothes off and put those wool warm-ups on and we were out there three hours. I ran up and down that lane maybe 150 times while they took pictures. I'd jump in the car and try to get warm. I'll bet they took over 150 pictures and that's how they got the cover."

The cover and story turned out to be a boon for Mount and Indiana high school basketball. "I think state-wide I was pretty well known at that point," he said. "That cover and story put me on the map nationally. Fathers and grandparents will bring their kids to my basketball camp and they'll always mention that article."

In March, 2005, Mike Warren, who played on two of John Wooden's record 10 NCAA Division I championship teams at UCLA, accompanied the Hoosier legend from California to South Bend for the McDonald's All-American High School Game festivities at Notre Dame.

"That was really special," said Warren, a South Bend native. "Wooden is on the McDonald's advisory board and since the game was in South Bend, he decided I might like to go back home. I jumped at the opportunity." Wooden, who coached at South Bend Central from 1934 to 1943, and Warren, who played at Central, went to a luncheon on the Notre Dame campus for people who played for Wooden either in high school or college.

Warren says Wooden loves to laugh. "He's not always as serious as people might think. When you consider all the things that he has accomplished, and all the accolades and awards he has earned over the years, I don't know too many people who can remain as level-headed and as humble as he has remained."

Mike has the rights to Wooden's life story and hopes to make a movie of the man from Martinsville. "I have a writer and we're in the beginning stages," said Mike. "We pray that it's going to be a feature film. But we're looking at a couple of years down the road. Coach's impact on basketball all across Indiana is amazing. What he's done for basketball in Indiana and California is immeasurable."

Billy and Dave Shepherd of Carmel are the only brothers ever to be named Mr. Basketball in separate years. Billy Shepherd was the 1968 Mr. Basketball. Dave received the honor in 1970. Dave played one year with Billy under their father as coach of the Greyhounds and he loves to tell the story of his first varsity game.

"I was having a real good game against Westfield," he said, chuckling. "At the end of the third quarter I think I had like 24 points, eight or 10 rebounds and three or four assists. I think Billy had about 20 points.

"I was getting ready to go out for the fourth quarter and I was all fired up. Scott Richards, one of our subs, taps me on the shoulder and says, 'I'm in for you.' I said, 'What? In for me?' I learned fast that no sophomore is going to come in and outscore Billy Shepherd in the first game of his career. I sat out the fourth quarter and watched Billy put on a little show. He ended up with

30. Of course, I ended up with 24. Big Bill taught me a lesson. Here's how it is, kid. You'll have your chance later on, but right now that's not how the program's set up."

Dave says his favorite story of that sophomore season was "telling that Billy and I combined for 88 points one night. They say, 'You gotta be kidding. You and Billy scored 88 points?' Yeah, I say, he got 70 and I got 18." That 70 is the Carmel one-game record. In Dave's senior season he scored 66 against Frankfort in a home game. "My dad took me out with about 2 minutes left and the fans went crazy. He put me back in. I told him it was a little late. I wound up with 66. I always tell people, 'It's hard to believe a guy gets 66 points in a high school basketball game and not have the school record.'"

When Chuck DeVoe, who played high school basketball at Indianapolis' Park School before it became known as Park Tudor, was at Princeton, he was involved in two bittersweet games against Ivy League foe Columbia.

"We had the longest winning streak in the country my junior year (1950-51) and Columbia was right behind us, also being undefeated," said DeVoe. "We had a play set up out of bounds. It was to go to me. The play worked perfectly, but I blew a layup with about 20 seconds to go. We got the rebound and I had the ball stolen from me. A guy took it down the floor and scored as the game ended. Columbia won by one point.

"About 20 years later I was tapped on the shoulder at Detroit Diesel Allison in Indianapolis. I turned around and the guy said, 'You don't remember me.' I said, 'No, I don't think so.' He said, 'I'm the guy from Columbia who stole the ball from you.' The guy's name was Bob Sullivan."

In DeVoe's senior season, Princeton won the Ivy League and qualified for the NCAA tournament. The Tigers played Columbia twice. Jack Molinas was Columbia's star player. "Molinas burned us real bad in the first game at Columbia," said DeVoe. "In the second game I guarded him and held him down quite a bit. I always was very proud of that. I always thought that was the best defensive game I ever played, until the news broke about Molinas shaving points all through his college career and becoming the master fixer. It was like the air went out of the balloon." Molinas was later killed, reportedly by the mob.

George McGinnis, who led Indianapolis Washington High School to the 1969 state championship and then was named Mr. Basketball, always seems to be smiling. "I am who I am," he said. "I never try to portray myself as anything other than what I am. I don't think I've changed much in terms of personality.

"A speech teacher at Washington had a profound effect on me. I remember the time I was a sophomore when Channel 13 came out and did a report on our team. They brought me over to say a few words and the guy put the microphone to my mouth and I just froze.

"My speech teacher saw that TV clip that night. She called me in the next day and said, 'If you want to be an athlete, and you're going to be out there in the public eye, you need to learn to speak properly. If you're willing, I'll spend some individual time with you after school.' We became great friends. I went home with her and we did little things, and I got up and I did speeches. It was people like that who really made a difference, who set the base for you. She didn't have to do that, but she took time out of her life to help somebody."

An eight-column headline in the *Evansville Courier* of March 22, 1948 read: "Bears Are Welcomed Home By 4000 Fans At Central Gym." Lee Hamilton, former U.S. House of Representatives member from southern Indiana, remembers well the homecoming his Evansville Central High School team received after finishing runner-up in the state tournament.

"I was not able to walk," said Hamilton, who suffered a severe knee injury in the morning round of the state finals at Butler Fieldhouse (now Hinkle Fieldhouse). "I came in on crutches. We came by bus from Indianapolis and I remember we had a stop in Petersburg, Indiana, where a very large number of people came out to see us.

"In those days one of the interesting things was that the college game had not really taken hold yet. This was right after World War II. The NBA I don't think was even in existence. At least it was not prominent. So all of the sports energy, if you would, focused on high school basketball. For a town like Evansville it was THE big event.

"Today you've got Indiana University, you've got the NCAA, you've got the NBA, and you've got a lot of other things. It was a very different environment back then. Veterans were just coming back from World War II and the sports leagues had not really gotten underway, although the IHSAA was well organized. But the attention that the town (Evansville) gave to basketball and to basketball players was just extraordinary. We had the kind of attention you would give to an Indiana University national contender today."

Hallie Bryant, whose basketball career has extended from Indianapolis' Crispus Attucks High School to Indiana University to the Harlem Globetrotters and beyond, says players like Oscar Robertson and Larry Bird might have been gifted. More important, in Bryant's estimation, is that they both paid the price to be great.

"Yes, I paid the price in my career," said Hallie, and that's how the other 38 players profiled in this book got to enjoy so many glory days in basketball.